Razi's Tradition

(Abū Bakr Muḥammad
ibn Zakarīyā al-Rāzī)

Translated from the Arabic by

A. J. Arberry

IBS, Damascus, Syria

Islamic Book Service
POB 15744-2345
Damascus, Syria

CONTENTS

INTRODUCTION

RHAZES, "undoubtedly the greatest physician of the Islamic world and one of the great physicians of all time ",[1] was born at Raiy, near modern Teheran, in A.D. 864, and died there in A.D. 925. As is the case with many of the most famous Arab scholars and writers, comparatively little authentic is known of the details of his life ; for the Arabs of old were curiously incurious about the private affairs of their great men of learning, it being sufficient for them to know that they had composed valuable books and carried forward the frontiers of science and letters. Rhazes (this is the latinized form of his name, which was in full Abū Bakr Muhammad ibn Zakarīyā al-Rāzī) is said to have come to the study of medicine somewhat late in life ; according to most authorities, he devoted his earlier years to alchemy, mathematics, philosophy and literature. One biographer relates that "in his youth, he played on the lute and cultivated vocal music, but, on reaching the age of manhood, he renounced these occupations, saying that music proceeding from between mustachoes and a beard had no charms to recommend it ".[2]

Whenever it was that he turned his mind to more serious things—a respectable authority puts this event in the thirties of Rhazes' life [3]—certainly Baghdad was the city where he learned his medicine. By this time, the capital of the Abbasid Empire

[1] M. Meyerhof in *Legacy of Islam*, p. 323.
[2] Ibn Khallikān, *Biographical Dictionary* (transl. De Slane), III, p. 312.
[3] Ibn Abī Usaibi'a, I, p. 309. Ibn Khallikān, *loc. cit.*, says "over forty ".

I

had firmly established itself as the leading centre of learning in the known world. Successive rulers, from al-Manṣūr (754–75) and Hārūn al-Rashīd (d. 809) to al-Ma'mūn (813–33), had liberally endowed institutes for the study of the ancient Greek sciences; the writings of Plato, Aristotle, Plotinus, Hippocrates, Galen, Euclid, Oribasius, Paul of Aegina and many other philosophers, mathematicians and physicians were translated into Arabic, chiefly by the Christian Hunain ibn Ishāq (809–77) and his school. The family of Bukht-Yishū', likewise Christians, enjoyed the confidence of their Muslim masters because of their supreme skill in medicine and surgery. When Rhazes came to Baghdad he would have found there fully-equipped hospitals, well-stocked libraries, and a sound tradition of teaching and research. It is said that he studied there under a pupil of the great Hunain who was acquainted with Greek, Persian and Indian medicine [1]; some give the name of 'Alī ibn Rabban al-Tabarī as his teacher, the author of a celebrated book entitled *The Paradise of Wisdom*,[2] but this is impossible because al-Tabarī was dead before Rhazes came to Baghdad.

Rhazes presently returned to his birthplace in order to enter the service of the local ruler, and having already achieved a wide reputation as a physician he was given charge of the new hospital there. Later he went back to Baghdad, and directed a great hospital in the capital.[3] Thereafter he is stated to have travelled extensively and enjoyed the patronage of a number of royal masters. He composed a very great number of books, especially

[1] *Legacy of Islam*, p. 323.

[2] Ibn Khallikān, *loc. cit.*

[3] According to the authority quoted by Ibn Abī Usaibi'a, this was the great hospital established by the Buyid ruler 'Adud al-Daula; but Ibn Abī Usaibi'a rightly remarks that Rhazes lived long before 'Adud al-Daula, and indeed the hospital named after the latter was not completed until 978, see *Encylopaedia of Islam*, I, p. 143.

on medicine ; his most celebrated works being the *Kitāb
al-Mansūrī*, dedicated to and named after Abū Sālih al-Mansūr
ibn Ishāq ibn Ahmad ibn Nūh, prince of Kirman and Khurasan,[1]
the *Kitāb al-Mulūkī*, written in honour of 'Alī ibn Wēh-Sūdhān
of Tabaristan, and the *Hāwī*, a gigantic encyclopaedia which
was unfinished at Rhazes' death and was edited by his pupils,
it is said at the instance of Ibn al-'Amīd (d. 970), the vizier of
the Buyid ruler Rukn al-Daula, who recovered the notebooks
containing the rough draft from Rhazes' sister.[2]

Many anecdotes are related to illustrate Rhazes' pre-eminence
as a physician. Of these, one is chosen for reproduction here ;
not that one can have absolute confidence in its authenticity—
for its chronology raises difficulties—but nevertheless it gives
an attractive and probably accurate picture of the character of
the great sage, and of his royal patrons.

> Another of the House of Sāmān, Amīr Mansūr b. Nūh b. Nasr,
> became afflicted with an ailment which grew chronic, and remained
> established, and the physicians were unable to cure it. So the Amīr
> Mansūr sent messengers to summon Muhammad b. Zakariyyā of Ray
> to treat him. Muhammad b. Zakariyyā came as far as the Oxus, but
> when he saw it he said : "I will not embark in the boat ; God Most
> High saith, *Do not cast yourselves into peril with your own hands* ; and,
> again, it is surely a thing remote from wisdom voluntarily to place
> one's self in so hazardous a position." Ere the Amīr's messenger had
> gone to Bukhara and returned, he had composed a treatise entitled
> *Mansūrī*. So when a notable arrived with a special led-horse, bringing
> a message intermingled with promises of reward, he handed this

---

[1] Ibn Khallikān, III, p. 313 ; *Encycl. of Islam*, III, p. 256. The tradition
that the book was dedicated to the Samanid ruler Abū Sālih al-Mansūr
ibn Nūh involves an anachronism, for that prince did not come to the
throne until 961, long after Rhazes' death.
[2] Ibn Abī Usaibi'a, I, p. 314.

Mansūrī to him, saying : " I am this book, and by this book thou canst attain thine object, so that there is no need of me."

When the book reached the Amīr he was in grievous suffering wherefore he sent a thousand dinars and one of his own private horses, saying : " Strive to move him by all these kind attentions, but, if they prove fruitless, bind his hands and feet, place him in the boat, and fetch him across." So, just as the Amīr had commanded, they urgently entreated Muhammad b. Zakariyyā, but to no purpose. Then they bound his hands and feet, placed him in the boat, and, when they had ferried him across the river, released him. Then they brought the led-horse, fully caparisoned, before him, and he mounted in the best of humours, and set out for Bukhara. And when they enquired of him, saying, " We feared to bring thee across the water lest thou shouldst cherish enmity against us, but thou didst not so, nor do we see thee vexed in heart," he replied : " I know that every year several thousand persons cross the Oxus without being drowned, and that I too should probably not be drowned ; still, it was possible that I might perish, and if this had happened they would have continued till the Resurrection to say, A foolish fellow was Muhammad b. Zakariyyā, in that, of his own free will, he embarked in a boat and so was drowned. But when they bound me, I escaped all danger of censure ; for then they would say, They bound the poor fellow's hands and feet, so that he was drowned. Thus should I have been excused, not blamed, in case of my being drowned."

When they reached Bukhara, he saw the Amīr and began to treat him, exerting his powers to the utmost, but without relief to the patient. One day he came in before the Amīr and said : " To-morrow I am going to try another method of treatment, but for the carrying out of it you will have to sacrifice such-and-such a horse and such-and-such a mule," the two being both animals of note, so that in one night they had gone forty parasangs.

So next day he took the Amīr to the hot bath of Jū-yi-Mūliyān, outside the palace, leaving that horse and mule ready equipped and tightly girt in the charge of his own servant ; while of the King's retinue and attendants he suffered not one to enter the bath. Then he brought the King into the middle of the hot bath, and poured over him warm water, after which he prepared a draught and gave it to him to drink. And he kept him there till such time as the humours in his joints were matured.

Then he himself went out and put on his clothes, and, taking a knife in his hand, came in, and stood for a while reviling the King saying : "Thou didst order me to be bound and cast into the boat, and didst conspire against my life. If I do not destroy thee as a punishment for this, I am not Muhammad b. Zakariyyā."

The Amīr was furious, sprang from his place, and, partly from anger, partly from fear of the knife and dread of death, rose to his feet. When Muhammad b. Zakariyyā saw the Amīr on his feet he turned round and went out from the bath, and he and his servant mounted, the one the horse, the other the mule, and turned their faces towards the Oxus. At the time of the second prayer they crossed the river, and halted nowhere till they reached Merv. When Muhammad b. Zakariyyā reached Merv, he alighted, and wrote a letter to the Amīr, saying : "May the life of the King be prolonged in health of body and effective command ! According to agreement this servant treated his master, doing all that was possible. There was, however, an extreme weakness in the natural caloric, and the treatment of the disease by ordinary means would have been a protracted affair. I therefore abandoned it, and carried you to the hot bath for psychical treatment, and administered a draught, and left you so long as to bring about a maturity of the humours. Then I angered the King, so that an increase in the natural caloric was produced, and it gained strength until those humours, already softened, were dissolved. But henceforth it is not expedient that a meeting should take place between myself and the King."

Now after the Amīr had risen to his feet and Muhammad b. Zakariyyā had gone out, the Amīr sat down and at once fainted. When he came to himself he went forth from the bath and called to his servants, saying, "Where has the physician gone?" They answered, "He came out from the bath, and mounted the horse, while his attendant mounted the mule, and went off."

Then the Amīr knew what object he had in view. So he came forth on his own feet from the hot bath ; and tidings of this ran through the city, and his servants and retainers and people rejoiced greatly, and gave alms, and offered sacrifices, and held high festival. But they could not find the physician, seek him as they might. And on the seventh day Muhammad b. Zakariyyā's servant arrived, riding the horse and leading the mule, and presented the letter. The Amīr read it, and was astonished, and excused him, and sent him a horse, and a robe of honour, and equipment, and a cloak, and arms, and a turban, and a male slave, and a handmaiden ; and further commanded that there should be assigned to him in Ray from the settled estates a yearly allowance of two thousand dinars and two hundred ass-loads of corn. These marks of honour he forwarded to him by the hand of a trusty messenger, together with his apologies. So the Amīr completely regained his health, and Muhammad b. Zakariyyā attained his object.[1]

It would be attractive to conjecture that the *Spiritual Physick*, which was certainly composed for the same ruler as the *Mansūrī*, was written as a result of this encounter, to explain in greater detail the scientific principles underlying the psychological treatment which Rhazes had adopted with such complete success.

All our sources agree that in his later years Rhazes was smitten by cataract, and became quite blind. When he was urged to submit to cupping, he is said to have replied, " No, I have seen the world so long that I am tired of it."[2] Confirmatory evidence of his failing sight is furnished by Rhazes' autobiography, to which reference will presently be made. The spirit in which he faced death is illustrated by some verses he is reported to have composed in his old age.[3]

[1] Nizāmī, *Chahār Maqāla* (transl. E. G. Browne), pp. 115–18.
[2] Al-Qiftī, p. 179.
[3] Ibn Abī Usaibiʻa, I, p. 315.

Truly I know not—and decay
Hath laid his hand upon my heart,
And whispered to me that the day
Approaches, when I must depart—
I know not whither I shall roam,
Or where the spirit, having sped
From this its wasted fleshly home,
Will after dwell, when I am dead.

Rhazes is described as a man with a " great, scaly head ",
generous and gracious in his dealings with others, and most
compassionate towards the poor, whom he treated free of
charge and even maintained out of his own purse. His lectures
were thronged by students, and arranged in such a fashion that
several junior and senior lecturers dealt with any inquiries which
they were competent to answer, only referring to him matters
which passed their range of knowledge.[1]
The foregoing is the sum of what we are told about Rhazes
by Arab and Persian biographers, apart from monumental lists
of the titles of his books. A fortunate chance has preserved for
us a little tract in which he set about in his later days to justify
the manner of life he had lived, and the direction of his studies ;
and from these pages we are able to reconstruct a far clearer
image of the man than anything these unsatisfying sources can
supply.[2]
Rhazes' medical writings were highly prized in the Middle
Ages, alike by Muslims, Jews and Christians, and were accepted
as the basis for modern research. His *Hāwī* was translated into
Latin under the title *Continens* by the Sicilian Jew Faraj ibn
Sālim (Farragut) in 1279 ; the gigantic version was printed in

[1] Al-Qiftī, p. 179.
[2] *Al-Sīrat al-falsafīya* (ed. P. Kraus) : see selections from this work
quoted at the end of the preface.

its entirety five times between 1488 and 1542. The *Kitāb al-Mansūrī* ("Liber Almansoris", the companion of the present work) and *Kitāb al-Mulūkī* ("Liber Regius") were also published in Latin and cherished by medieval physicians as among their most precious works of reference. His monograph *On Smallpox and Measles* was printed in various translations some forty times between 1498 and 1866, and has been praised by modern doctors for its clinical accuracy.[1] With the possible exception of Avicenna and Averroes, whose influence was in any case philosophical rather than scientific, no man so powerfully affected the course of learning in the Middle Ages and the early Renaissance as Rhazes. It is scarcely surprising that Chaucer's *Doctor of Physic* should have included him in his impressive list of authorities.

> Well know he the old Esculapius,
> And Dioscorides, and eke Rufus ;
> Old Hippocras, Hali, and Gallien ;
> Serapion, Rasis, and Avicen ;
> Averrois, Damascene, and Constantin ;
> Bernard, and Gatisden, and Gilbertin.

His philosophical writings were never so widely known, chiefly because they were condemned as heretical by almost all Muslim opinion. Even the illustrious Abū Raihān al-Bīrūnī, the historian of India and broad-minded investigator of Indian philosophy and religion, added his voice to the general chorus of disapproval. Though he wrote a catalogue of Rhazes' works extant in his day, amounting to 184 items, and confessed that in his youth he was carried away by his enthusiasm for study to the point of reading Rhazes' *Metaphysica*, he roundly condemned him for dabbling in freethought, and even spoke of his blindness

[1] M. Meyerhof, *op. cit., loc. cit.*

as a Divine retribution.[1] Ibn Hazm, who composed a massive
work on sects and heresies, singled out Rhazes for particular
rejection.[2] So much for the orthodox ; even the Ismailis,
renegades that they were, disowned his philosophical teaching,
and Nāsir-i Khusrau the poet [3] and Hamīd al-Dīn al-Kirmānī
the theologian [4] applied themselves energetically to refuting
him. Orthodox and unorthodox were alike shocked most of
all by Rhazes' book *On Prophecy*—which, needless to say, has
not survived—in which he seems to have maintained the thesis
that reason is superior to inspiration, a view naturally intolerable
to any devout Muslim.

The *Spiritual Physick*, which is here offered in the first translation to be made into any language, belongs rather to the
realm of popular ethics than to that of high philosophy ; yet it
enables us to obtain a clear view of the background of Rhazes'
thought, and even to glimpse those dangerous propositions
which brought down on his head the execrations of the faithful.
The book is preserved in several manuscripts, and was first
studied in modern times by the Dutch orientalist De Boer.[5]
The *editio princeps* was published in 1939 by the late Paul Kraus,[6]
a most able and promising scholar, a victim of Nazi persecution,
who committed suicide at Cairo during the recent war. His
premature death was a severe blow to learning : the present
translation is put out as a small tribute to his memory.

Rhazes, as the list of his writings suggests, and the *Spiritual*

[1] Al-Bīrūnī, *Risāla* (ed. P. Kraus), pp. 3–5.
[2] Ibn Hazm, *al-Fasl fi 'l-milal*, I, pp. 24–33.
[3] Nāsir-i Khusrau, *Zād al-musāfirīn*, pp. 72 ff.
[4] Al-Kirmānī, *al-Aqwāl al-dhahabīya*, quoted by P. Kraus in his edition
of Rhazes.
[5] De Boer, *De " Medicina Mentis " van Arts Razi*.
[6] At Cairo, under the title *Rhagensis (Razis) Opera Philosophica*,
pp. 1–96.

Physick and *Autobiography* (among other works) amply prove, was thoroughly at home with the books of the Greek philosophers and physicians. He wrote for instance a commentary on Plato's *Timaeus*,[1] an epitome of Aristotle's writings on logic,[2] a refutation of Porphyry,[3] and epitomes of Hippocrates' *Aphorisms* [4] and of the medical works of Galen and Plutarch.[5] He was familiar besides with Oribasius, Aetius and Paul of Aegina, and was unquestionably well grounded in the entire canon of Greek works translated by Hunain ibn Ishāq and his school.   His studies of Arabic literature are attested not only by the admirable fluency and eloquence with which he uses the language, but also by the apt poetical quotations which flavour his discourse ; the present book contains an anecdote which proves his familiarity with the mentality and technical vocabulary of the Arab grammarians.   He writes like a master, and his style has the unmistakable ring of a man confident in the supremacy of his own reason and erudition.   His spirit of rational inquiry is entirely Greek ; his Persian blood is proved by his fondness for anecdote, besides innumerable little nuances of thought and expression.   His attitude of tolerant agnosticism anticipates the more celebrated outlook of another Persian scientist who in modern times has achieved universal fame and popularity—Omar Khayyám.

In the *Autobiography* Rhazes rejects the " early life " of Socrates—the inaccurate legend that he refused all pleasures, eschewed all human intercourse, and lived in a barrel in the wilderness—but approves of his " later life " when he is said to have married, begat children, and even taken up arms against the enemy.   In that essay, as in the *Spiritual Physick*, he revolts

[1] No. 107 in al-Bīrūnī's list.   [2] No. 91 in al-Bīrūnī.
[3] No. 128 in al-Bīrūnī.   [4] No. 112 in al-Bīrūnī.
[5] Nos. 108-11, 113 in al-Bīrūnī.

against the unreasonable austerities of monks and anchorites, and takes the view that God is far too compassionate to impose upon human beings burdens heavier than they can bear. Regarding the immortality of the soul he appears to reserve judgment, though he quotes freely Plato's opinion and outlines the psychological analysis of the *Timaeus*. His theory of pleasure—that it consists of a return to the state of nature—is based on the *Philebus*. When he writes on the fear of death, we seem to catch many echoes of the Epicurean teaching which Lucretius immortalized in a famous passage of the *De Natura Rerum*. Rhazes' general attitude might be summed up as one of intellectual hedonism ; though its origins in classical philosophy are obvious, it reflects very characteristically the outlook of the cultured Persian gentleman, constantly down the ages informing Iranian thought and life.

The *Spiritual Physick* appears therefore as the product of a curiously perfect blend of two civilizations, expressed in the language of a third ; an admirable synthesis of science and metaphysics, shaped in the mind of a master physician and given verbal form by a master of language. It is scarcely an exaggeration to say that the book is unique in Arabic literature. The author hardly betrays himself as a Muslim, though his name Muhammad proves him so to have been ; otherwise he would have done as all other Arabs did who wrote on ethics, elaborating his discourse with quotations from the Koran and the sayings of the Prophet, and only introducing the views of Greek thinkers where they appeared to accord with sound Islamic teaching. Avicenna was much more orthodox ; he even wrote commentaries on parts of the Koran.

Rhazes' God is a very rational and reasonable God, a God, we might almost say, with a sense of humour, an eminently Persian God. When we lay down this book, we feel that we have been in the presence of a man who knew no vain fear because he had analysed fear out of his mind ; a man who knew no vain hope because he knew that the laws of nature were as beneficent as they were immutable ; a man indifferent to fame and wealth because he was intellectually persuaded of their worthlessness ; a man whose counsel is a sure guide through the baffling perplexities that are the inevitable accompaniment of human life, a sage and reasonable comfort under the dark shadows of extreme affliction and death.

To conclude these prefatory remarks, we here append some passages drawn from Rhazes' defence of the philosophic life, so that we may leave the reader with the voice of the author himself speaking. He begins the *Autobiography* by stating the charge that unnamed critics had brought against him.

Certain men of a speculative turn, discriminating and of undoubted attainments, having observed that we consort with our fellows and engage in various manners of earning a livelihood, reproach us on this account, finding it to be detrimental in us and asserting that we are swerving aside from the philosophic life.

The criticism is particularly levelled at his alleged failure to live up to the ideals of Socrates, his confessed master, who is pictured as living a life of utmost rigour ; at the same time Socrates himself is criticized—according to this legend—for conduct contrary to the laws of nature and liable to lead to the extinction of the human race and the desolation of the world. Rhazes agrees with the objection that is raised to Socrates' " earlier life ", but makes it clear that he differs from his master " only quantitively, not qualitatively " ; he is in full agreement with the view that life should be lived in a disciplined manner, but cannot accept the doctrine of extreme self-abnegation. He argues the proposition that pleasure is not to be indulged when it is irrational in its appeal, much along the same lines as in the *Spiritual Physick*. Then he turns to the problem of pain.

Since we have laid it down as the foundation of our case that our Lord and Ruler is kindly and compassionate towards us and regards us with loving care, it follows from this that He hates that any pain should befall us ; it also follows that whatever happens to us not of our own earning and choosing but due to some necessity of nature, is to be regarded as inevitable. It therefore behoves us not to pain any sentient creature whatsoever, unless it deserves to be pained, or unless it be to avert from it still greater pain.

Rhazes follows up the implications of this conclusion by condemning blood sports except when practised against carnivorous beasts such as lions, tigers and wolves ; at the same time he urges the annihilation of snakes, scorpions and other noisome creatures that have no discoverable beneficial use or property. From the animal kingdom he turns back to man.

Since it is prohibited by the verdict of reason and justice alike for any man to inflict pain upon another, it follows from this that he should not inflict pain upon himself either. Many things come under this general observation as being rejected by the arbitrament of reason— for instance, the Indian way of propitiating God by burning the body and casting it down upon sharp spikes, or the Manichean practice of self-mutilation to overcome the sexual urge, excessive fasting, and defiling oneself by washing in urine. The same heading also includes— though at a much lower level—the monasticism and hermit-life taken up by some Christians, and the fashion followed by many Muslims of spending their whole time at mosque, declining to earn their living, and contenting themselves with little and unappetizing food and rough, uncomfortable clothes.

The practice of austerity is obviously easier for those not accustomed to luxury from birth than for the children of rich parents ; the latter cannot be required to compete with the former in this respect on a basis of equality.

But the boundary which cannot be transgressed is that they should refrain from such pleasures as may not be attained save by perpetrating cruelty and murder—in short, all those things that provoke the wrath of God and are forbidden by the verdict of reason and justice.

This is what Rhazes calls the "upper limit" of discipline which he holds to be obligatory for all men to respect; to keep above the "lower limit" is equally important.

This means that a man should eat such food as will not harm him or make him ill, while not exceeding this to partake of such delicious and appetising dishes as are desired for the mere gratification of pleasure and greed, and not to allay hunger; that he should wear such clothes as his skin can tolerate without discomfort, not hankering after fine and flowery raiment; and that he should seek such a dwelling-place as may shelter him from excessive heat and cold, not going beyond this to look for magnificent residences painted up in fine colours and lavishly ornamented; unless indeed he possesses such ample means that he can afford to maintain this style without injustice or aggression towards others and without exerting himself unduly to earn the wherewithal.

Such are the two extremes within which it behoves the philosopher to confine himself.

Since the Creator is Omniscient and All-Just, since He is absolute knowledge and justice and mercy, and since He is our Creator and Ruler and we are His creatures and subjects; whereas that servant is most beloved by his master who the most closely follows his master's lead and example, it follows that the creature nearest to God's favour is he who is the most knowing, the justest, the most merciful and compassionate. This indeed is what the philosophers meant· when they said that the purpose of philosophy was "to make oneself like to God, to the greatest extent possible to man." [1] That is the sum total of the philosophic life.

[1] A quotation from Plato, *Theaetetus*, 176 b.

Rhazes refers his readers to the *Spiritual Physick* for a detailed explanation of his argument ; then he concludes his defence as follows.

Now that we have explained what we desired to set forth in this place, we will go back to set out what we have to say in reply to our critics ; declaring that by God's help and assistance we have up to this very day in no way conducted ourselves in a manner meriting our expulsion from the title of philosopher. For only those men deserve to have their names expunged from the roll of philosophy who have fallen short in both branches of philosophy—the theoretical and the practical—together, either through ignorance of what a philosopher should know, or out of failure to conduct their lives as a philosopher ought. We, God be praised and thanked for His assistance and guidance, are innocent of such failure.

To take theory : if we possessed only so much strength of knowledge as was necessary to compose this present book, that alone would suffice to prevent our name from being expunged from the roll of philosophy ; not to mention our other writings [Rhazes here adds a considerable list of titles] which amount in all to approximately two hundred items, reckoning in books, pamphlets and essays, down to the time of making this present pamphlet ; writings which cover all branches of philosophy, physical and metaphysical alike. As for mathematics, I freely concede that I have only looked into this subject to the extent that was absolutely indispensable, not wasting my time upon refinements ; of set purpose, not out of incapacity for the study. If any man wishes to have my excuse on this head, I make bold to assert that the right course is in fact that which I have followed, not the one adopted by some so-called philosophers who fritter away their whole lives indulging in geometrical superfluities. If therefore the amount of knowledge I possess is not sufficient for me to deserve the name of philosopher, I should very much like to know who of my contemporaries is so qualified.

Now as to the practical side : by God's help and succour I have never in all my life transgressed the twain limits which I have defined, nor have I committed any act so far as I am aware that would justify my conduct being called unphilosophical. I have never kept the ruler's company in the way of bearing arms or undertaking the control of affairs ; my service has been confined to that of a physician and a courtier charged with two responsibilities—to treat and restore him when he was sick, and when he was well to win his confidence and offer him counsel ; and in counselling him, let God be my witness, I have only advised such actions as I hoped would prove beneficial both to him and to his subjects. I have never been observed to be greedy to amass wealth, or to be extravagant in spending it ; I have not been forward to quarrel and dispute with my fellows, or to oppress them—on the contrary, it is well known that I have always acted in the very opposite manner, to the point of sacrificing many of my own rights for the sake of others.

As for my habits of eating and drinking, and my amusements, those who have observed me frequently will be aware that I have never been guilty of excess or extravagance in these, any more than in regard to my clothes, my mount, my servants and handmaidens.

My love and passion for knowledge, and my labours to acquire the same, are familiar to all who have kept my company or seen me at my studies ; from my youth up to this very time, I have not ceased to devote myself to this object. If ever I have come upon a book I have not read, or heard tell of a man I have not met, I have not turned aside to any engagement whatever—even though it has been to my great loss—before mastering that book or learning all that man knew. So great in fact have been my endeavours and endurance, that in a single year I have written as many as 20,000 pages in a script as minute as that used for amulets. I was engaged fifteen years upon my great compendium, working night and day, until my sight began to fail and the nerves of my hand were paralysed, so that at the present time I am prevented from reading and writing ; even so I do not give up these occupations so far as I am able, but always enlist the help of someone to read and write for me.

If the amount of my accomplishments in all these matters is still regarded by my critics as disqualifying me from occupying the rank of a philosopher in practice, and if their conception of the purpose of following the philosophic life is other than what we have described, let them state their charge against us, either verbally or in writing. Then, if they can prove superior knowledge, we will accept their verdict; on the other hand, if we can establish any error or weakness in their case, we will refute it. Or let me be lenient with them; let me acknowledge that I have been wanting on the practical side; yet what have they to say on the side of theory? If they find me deficient in this respect too, they only have to state their case and we will examine it; if they are right, we will submit, and if they are wrong, we will reject their charge. But if they do not hold me inadequate on the theoretical side, the best they can do is to profit of my theory, and pay no heed to my personal conduct, remembering what the poet has said:

> Practise what I have preached; and if there be
> In what I practised some deficiency,
> Yet thou canst profit of my theory,
> And my shortcomings will not injure thee.

PREFACE

GOD give the Prince perfect happiness and complete bliss.—
Mention having been made in the presence of the Prince (God
give him long life !) of a treatise I compiled upon the reformation of the character, that had been required of me by certain
of my brethren in Baghdad during my sojourn there, my Lord
the Prince (may God assist him !) commanded me to compose
a book that should contain the chief points of this subject, to be
as brief and concise as possible, and to entitle it the *Spiritual
Physick* ; that it might be a companion to the *Liber Almansoris* [1]
(whose purpose is the Bodily Physick) and correspond therewith ; for he estimated (God prolong his power !) that if it
were joined to the other, general profit would be the result, as
comprehending both the soul and the flesh.

I therefore applied myself to this task, and promoted it before
all my other occupations ; and I pray that God may so assist
me, that I shall please my Lord the Prince and win his favour
and approval. I have divided this book into twenty chapters,
as follows :

(1) Of the Excellence and Praise of Reason.

(2) Of Suppressing and Restraining the Passion, with a
Summary of the Views of Plato the Philosopher.

(3) Summary Prolegomena to the Detailed Account of Each
of the Evil Dispositions of the Soul.

(4) Of How a Man may Discover his Own Vices.

(5) Of Repelling Carnal Love and Familiarity, with a
Summary Account of Pleasure.

[1] *Kitāb al-Mansūrī*, see Introduction, pp. 3, 8.

(6) Of Repelling Conceit.
(7) Of Repelling Envy.
(8) Of Repelling Excessive and Hurtful Anger.
(9) Of Casting Away Mendacity.
(10) Of Casting Away Miserliness.
(11) Of Repelling Excessive and Hurtful Anxiety and Worry.
(12) Of Dismissing Grief.
(13) Of Repelling Greed.
(14) Of Repelling Habitual Drunkenness.
(15) Of Repelling Addiction to Sexual Intercourse.
(16) Of Repelling Excessive Fondness, Trifling, and Ritual.
(17) Of the Amount of Earning, Acquiring, and Expending.
(18) Of Repelling the Strife and Struggle in Quest of Worldly Rank and Station, and the Difference between the Counsel of Passion and Reason.
(19) Of the Virtuous Life.
(20) Of the Fear of Death.

The discrepancy between the wording of the chapter headings as given here, and that found in the body of the text, reflects the author's inconsistency in the original Arabic.

CHAPTER I

Of the Excellence and Praise of Reason

THE Creator (Exalted be His Name) gave and bestowed upon us Reason to the end that we might thereby attain and achieve every advantage, that lies within the nature of such as us to attain and achieve, in this world and the next. It is God's greatest blessing to us, and there is nothing that surpasses it in procuring our advantage and profit. By Reason we are preferred above the irrational beasts, so that we rule over them and manage them, subjecting and controlling them in ways profitable alike to us and them. By Reason we reach all that raises us up, and sweetens and beautifies our life, and through it we obtain our purpose and desire. For by Reason we have comprehended the manufacture and use of ships, so that we have reached unto distant lands divided from us by the seas ; by it we have achieved medicine with its many uses to the body, and all the other arts that yield us profit. By Reason we have comprehended matters obscure and remote, things that were secret and hidden from us ; by it we have learned the shape of the earth and the sky, the dimension of the sun, moon and other stars, their distances and motions ; by it we have achieved even the knowledge of the Almighty, our Creator, the most majestic of all that we have sought to reach and our most profitable attainment. In short, Reason is the thing without which our state would be the state of wild beasts, of children and lunatics ; it is the thing whereby we picture our intellectual acts before they become manifest to the senses, so that we see them exactly as though we had sensed them, then we represent these pictures in our sensual acts so that they correspond exactly with what we have represented and imagined.

Since this is its worth and place, its value and significance, it behoves us not to bring it down from its high rank or in any way to degrade it, neither to make it the governed seeing that it is the governor, or the controlled seeing that it is the controller, or the subject seeing that it is the sovereign ; rather must we consult it in all matters, respecting it and relying upon it always, conducting our affairs as it dictates and bringing them to a stop when it so commands. We must not give Passion the mastery over it, for Passion is the blemish of Reason, clouding it and diverting it from its proper path and right purpose, preventing the reasonable man from finding the true guidance and the ultimate salvation of all his affairs. Nay, but we must discipline and subject our Passion, driving and compelling it to obey the every dictate of Reason. If we do thus, our Reason will become absolutely clear and will illuminate us with all its light, bringing us to the achievement of all that we desire to attain ; and we shall be happy in God's free gift and grace of it.

CHAPTER II

Of Suppressing and Restraining the Passion, with a Summary of the Views of Plato the Philosopher

Now following on this we will proceed to speak about Spiritual Physick, the goal of which is the reformation of the soul's character ; and we propose to be extremely concise, going straight forward to deal with those points, principles and ideas which are the foundations of this entire object. We state that our intention in prefixing our views on Reason and Passion was because we considered this to be as it were the starting-point of our whole purpose ; we shall now follow it up with a discussion of the most important and loftiest fundamentals of this matter.

The loftiest and most important of these fundamentals, and that most helpful in reaching our object in the present book, is the suppression of passion, the opposing of natural inclinations in most circumstances, and the gradual training of the soul to that end. For this is the first point of superiority of man over the beasts—I mean the faculty of will, and the release of action after deliberation. This is because the beasts are undisciplined, and do whatever their natural inclinations dictate, acting without restraint or deliberation. You will not find that any undisciplined animal will refrain from defecating, or from seizing upon its food whenever it is there at hand and it feels the need of it, in the way you find a man leaving that on one side and compelling his inclinations to obedience at the dictate of various intellectual ideas ; on the contrary, the beasts act exactly as their instincts urge, without restraint or conscious choice.

This degree of superiority over the beasts, in the way of reining the natural impulses, belongs pretty well to the majority of men, even if it be as a result of training and education. It is general and universal, and may readily be observed on all hands, and in fact every child is accustomed to it and is brought up accordingly ; the point requires no labouring. At the same time there is a great difference and a wide range of variety between the different peoples in this respect. However, to reach the highest summit of this virtue attainable by human nature is scarcely open to any but the supreme philosopher ; such a man must be accounted as superior to the common run of humanity, as mankind as a whole excels the beasts in reining the natural instincts and controlling the passion. From this we realize that whosoever desires to adorn himself with this ornament, and to perfect this virtue in his soul, is upon a hard and difficult quest ; he needs to acclimatize himself to controlling and opposing and wrestling with his passion. And because there is a great difference and a wide range of variety between men as regards their temperaments, the acquisition of certain virtues rather than others and the getting rid of certain vices rather than others will prove a harder or an easier task for some men rather than the rest.

Now I will begin by mentioning how this virtue may be acquired—I mean the suppression and opposing of the passion— seeing that it is the loftiest and most important of these virtues, and its position relative to this entire purpose is similar to that of the element which immediately succeeds the origin.

Passion and instinct are always inciting and urging and pressing us to follow after present pleasures and to choose them without reflection or deliberation upon the possible consequence, even though this may involve pain hereafter and prevent us from attaining a pleasure many times greater than that immediately experienced. This is because they, our passion and instinct, see nothing else but the actual state in which they happen to be, and only seek to get rid of the pain that hurts them at that very moment. In this way a child suffering from ophthalmia will rub its eyes and eat dates and play in the sun. It therefore behoves the intelligent man to restrain and suppress his passion and instinct, and not to let them have their way except after careful and prudent consideration of what they may bring in their train ; he will represent this to himself and weigh the matter accurately, and then he will follow the course of greater advantage. This he will do, lest he should suffer pain where he supposed he would experience pleasure, and lose where he thought he would gain. If in the course of such representation and balancing he should be seized by any doubt, he will not give his appetite free play, but will continue to restrain and suppress it ; for he cannot be sure that in gratifying his appetite he will not involve himself in evil consequences very many times more painful and distressing than the labour of resolutely suppressing it. Prudence clearly dictates that he should deny such a lust. Again, if the two discomforts—that of suppression, and that consequent upon gratification—seem exactly balanced, he will still continue to suppress his appetite ; for the immediate bitterness is easier and simpler to taste than that which he must inevitably expect to swallow in the great majority of cases.

Nor is this enough. He ought further to suppress his passion in many circumstances even when he foresees no disagreeable consequence of indulgence, and that in order to train and discipline his soul to endure and become accustomed to such denial (for then it will be far less difficult to do so when the consequences are bad), as much as to prevent his lusts getting control of him and dominating him. The lusts in any case have sufficient hold, in the ordinary way of nature and human disposition, without needing to be reinforced by habit as well, so that a man will find himself in a situation where he cannot resist them at all.

You must know also that those who persistently indulge and gratify their appetites ultimately reach a stage where they no longer have any enjoyment of them, and still are unable to give them up. For instance, those who are forever having intercourse with women, or drinking, or listening to music—though these are the strongest and deepest-rooted of all the lusts—do not enjoy these indulgences so much as men who do not incessantly gratify them ; for these passions become for them exactly the same as any other passion with other men—that is to say, they become commonplace and habitual. Nevertheless it is not within their power to leave off these pursuits because they have turned into something of the nature of a necessity of life for them, instead of being a luxury and a relish. They are in consequence affected adversely in their religious life as well as their mundane situation, so that they are compelled to employ all kinds of shifts, and to acquire money by risking their lives and precipitating themselves into any sort of danger. In the end they find they are miserable where they expected to be happy, that they are sorrowful where they expected to rejoice, that they are pained where they expected to experience pleasure. So what difference is there between them and the man who deliberately sets out to destroy himself ? They are exactly like animals duped by the bait laid for them in the snares ; when they arrive in the trap, they neither obtain what they had been duped with nor are they able to escape from what they have fallen into.

This then will suffice as to the amount the appetites should be suppressed : they may only be indulged where it is known that the consequence will not involve a man in pain and temporal loss equivalent to the pleasure thereby obtained—much less discomfort superior to and exceeding the pleasure that is momentarily experienced. This is the view and assertion and recommendation even of those philosophers who have not considered the soul to have an independent existence, but to decay and perish with the body in which it is lodged. As for those who hold that the soul has an individual identity of its own, and that it uses the body as it would an instrument or an implement, not perishing simultaneously with it, they rise far, far beyond the mere reining of the instincts, and combating and opposing the passions. They despise and revile exceedingly those who allow themselves to be led by and who incline after their lower nature, considering them to be no better than beasts. They believe that by following and indulging their passion, by inclining after and loving their appetites, by regretting anything they may miss, and inflicting pain on animals in order to secure and satisfy their lusts, these men will experience, after the soul has left the body, pain and regret and sorrow for the evil consequences of their actions alike abundant and prolonged.

These philosophers can put forward the very physique of man to prove that he is not equipped to occupy himself with pleasures and lusts, seeing how deficient he is in this respect compared with the irrational animals, but rather to use his powers of thought and deliberation. For a single wild beast experiences more pleasure in eating and having intercourse than a multitude of men can possibly achieve ; while as for its capacity for casting care and thought aside, and enjoying life simply and wholly, that is a state of affairs no man can ever rival. This is because that is the animal's entire be-all and end-all ; we may observe that a beast at the very moment of its slaughter will still go on eating and drinking with complete absorption. They further argue that if the gratification of the appetites and the indulgence of the calls of nature had been the nobler part, man would never have been made so deficient in this respect or been more meanly endowed than the animals. The very fact that man is so deficient—in spite of his being the noblest of mortal animals—in his share of these things, whereas he possesses such an ample portion of deliberation and reflection, is enough to teach us that it is nobler to utilize and improve the reason, and not to be slave and lackey of the calls of nature.

Moreover, they say, if the advantage lay in gratifying carnal pleasure and lust, the creature furnished by nature to that end would be nobler than that not so equipped. By such a standard the bull and the ass would be superior not only to man, but also to the immortal beings, and to God Himself, Who is without carnal pleasure and lust.

It may be (they go on) that certain undisciplined men unused to reflect and deliberate upon such matters will not agree with us that the beasts enjoy greater pleasure than men. Those who argue thus may quote against us such an instance as that of a king who, having triumphed over an opposing foe, thenceforward sits at his amusement, and summons together and displays all his pomp and circumstance, so that he achieves the ultimate limit of what a man may reach. "What", they ask, "is the pleasure of a beast in comparison with the pleasure of such a man? Can so great a pleasure be measured or related with any other?" Those who speak in this fashion should realize that the perfection or imperfection of such pleasures must not be judged by comparing one pleasure with another, but in relation to the need felt for such a pleasure. Consider the case of a man who requires 1,000 dinars to put his affairs in order : if he is given 999, that will not completely restore his position for him. On the other hand suppose a man needs a single dinar : his situation will be perfectly amended by obtaining that one dinar. Yet the former has been given many times more than the latter, and still his state is not completely restored. When

c

a beast has enjoyed full satisfaction of the call of its instincts,
its pleasure therein is perfect and complete ; it feels no pain or
hurt at missing a still greater gratification because such an idea
never occurs to its mind at all. Yet in any case the beast always
experiences the superior pleasure ; for there is no man who can
ever attain all his hopes and desires, since his soul being endowed
with the faculties of reflection, deliberation, and imagination of
what he yet lacks, and it being in its nature always to consider
that the state enjoyed by another is bound to be superior, never
under any circumstances is it free from yearning and gazing after
what it does not itself possess, and from being fearful and anxious
lest it lose what it has possessed ; its pleasure and desire are
therefore always in a state of imperfect realization. If any man
should possess half the world, his soul would still wrestle with
him to acquire the remainder, and would be anxious and fearful
of losing hold of as much as it has already gotten ; and if he
possessed the entire world, nevertheless he would yearn for
perpetual well-being and immortality, and his soul would gaze
after the knowledge of all the mysteries of heaven and earth.
One day, as I have heard tell, someone spoke in the presence of
a great-souled king of the splendid and immortal joys of Paradise,
whereupon the king remarked, " Such bliss seems to me wholly
bitter and wearisome, when I reflect that if I were granted it,
I should be in the position of one on whom a favour and a kindness had been conferred." How could such a man ever know
perfect pleasure and enjoyment of his lot ? And who is there
that rejoices within himself, save only the beasts and those who
live like beasts ? So the poet says :

> Can any man be truly blest,
> Save him immortally possessed
> Of fortune, who has scarce a care
> And never goes to bed with fear ?

This sect of philosophers soar beyond the mere reining and opposing of passion, even beyond the contempt and mortification thereof, unto a matter exceedingly sublime. They partake of a bare subsistence of food and drink ; they acquire not wealth or lands or houses ; and some advance so far in this opinion that they go apart from other men, and withdraw into waste places. Such are the arguments they put forward in support of their views regarding the things that are present and seen. As for their reasonings about the state of the soul after it has left the body, to speak of this would take us far beyond the scope of the present book, alike in loftiness, length and breadth : in loftiness, because this involves research into the nature of the soul, the purpose of its association with and separation from the body, and its state after it has gone out of it ; in length, because each of these several branches of research requires its own interpretation and explanation, to an extent many times the discourse contained in this book ; and in breadth, because the purpose of such researches is the salvation of the soul after it has left the body, though it is true that the discourse involves a major consideration of the reformation of character. Still, there will be no harm in giving a very brief account of these matters, without however involving ourselves in an argument for or against their opinions ; what we have particularly in view are those ideas which we think will assist and enable us to fulfil the purpose of our present book.

Plato, the chief and greatest of the philosophers, held that there are three souls in every man. The first he called the rational and divine soul, the second the choleric and animal, and the third the vegetative, incremental and appetitive soul. The animal and vegetative souls were created for the sake of the rational soul. The vegetative soul was made in order to feed the body, which is as it were the instrument and implement of the rational soul ; for the body is not of an eternal, indissoluble substance, but its substance is fluid and soluble, and every soluble object only survives by leaving behind it something to replace that element which is dissolved. The choleric soul's function is to be of assistance to the rational soul in suppressing the appetitive soul and in preventing it from preoccupying the rational soul with its manifold desires so that it is incapable of using its reason. If the rational soul employed its reason completely, this would mean that it would be delivered from the body in which it is enmeshed. These two souls—the vegetative and the choleric—possess in Plato's view no special substance that survives the corruption of the body, such as that which belongs to the rational soul. On the contrary one of them, the choleric, is the entire temperament of the heart, while the other, the appetitive, is the entire temperament of the liver. As for the temperament of the brain, this he said is the first instrument and implement used by the rational soul.

Man is fed and derives his increase and growth from the liver, his heat and pulse-movement from the heart, his sensation, voluntary movement, imagination, thought and memory from the brain. It is not the case that this is part of its peculiar property and temperament ; it belongs rather to the essence dwelling within it and using it after the manner of an instrument or implement. However, it is the most intimate of all the instruments and implements associated with this agent.

Plato taught that men should labour by means of corporeal physick (which is the well-known variety) as well as spiritual physick (which is persuasion through arguments and proofs) to equilibrate the actions of the several souls so that they may neither fail nor exceed what is desired of them. Failure in the vegetative soul consists in not supplying food, growth and increase of the quantity and quality required by the whole body ; its excess is when it surpasses and transgresses that limit so that the body is furnished with an abundance beyond its needs, and plunges into all kinds of pleasures and desires. Failure in the choleric soul consists in not having the fervour, pride and courage to enable it to rein and vanquish the appetitive soul at such times as it feels desire, so as to come between it and its desires ; its excess is when it is possessed of so much arrogance and love of domination that it seeks to overcome all other men and the entire animal kingdom, and has no other ambition but supremacy and domination—such a state of soul as affected Alexander the Great. Failure in the rational soul is recognized when it does not occur to it to wonder and marvel at this world of ours, to meditate upon it with interest, curiosity and a passionate desire to discover all that it contains, and above all to investigate the body in which it dwells and its form and fate after death. Truly, if a man does not wonder and marvel at our world, if he is not moved to astonishment at its form, and if his soul does not gaze after the knowledge of all that it contains, if he is not concerned or interested to discover what his state will be after death, his portion of reason is that of the beasts—nay, of bats and fishes and worthless things that never think or reflect. Excess in the rational soul is proved when a man is so swayed and overmastered by the consideration of such things as these that the appetitive soul cannot obtain the food and sleep and so forth to keep the body fit, or in sufficient quantity to maintain the temperament of the brain in a healthy state. Such a man is forever seeking and probing and striving to the utmost of his powers, supposing that he will attain and realize these matters in a shorter time than that which is absolutely necessary for their achievement. The result is that the temperament of the whole body is upset, so that he falls a prey to depression and melancholia, and he misses his entire quest through supposing that he could quickly master it.

Plato held that the period which has been appointed for the survival of this dissoluble and corruptible body, in a state the rational soul can make use of to procure the needs of its salvation after it leaves the body—the period that is from the time a man is born until he grows old and withers—is adequate for the fulfilment of every man, even the stupidest ; provided he never gives up thinking and speculating and gazing after the matters we have mentioned as proper to the rational soul, and provided he despises this body and the physical world altogether, and loathes and detests it, being aware that the sentient soul, so long as it is attached to any part of it, continues to pass through states deleterious and painful because generation and corruption are forever succeeding each other in the body ; provided further that he does not hate but rather yearns to depart out of the body and to be liberated from it. He believed that when the time comes for the sentient soul to leave the body in which it is lodged, if it has acquired and believed firmly in these ideas it will pass immediately into its own world, and will not desire to be attached to any particle of the body thereafter ; it will remain living and reasoning eternally, free from pain, and rejoicing in its place of abode. For life and reason belong to it of its own essence ; freedom from pain will be the consequence of its removal from generation and corruption ; it will rejoice in its own world and place of abiding because it has been liberated from association with the body and existence in the physical world. But if the soul leaves the body without having acquired these ideas and without having recognized the true nature of the physical world, but rather still yearning after it and eager to exist therein, it will not leave its present dwelling-place but will continue to be linked with some portion of it ; it will not cease

—because of the succession of generation and corruption within the body in which it is lodged—to suffer continual and reduplicated pains, and cares multitudinous and afflicting.

Such in brief are the views of Plato, and of Socrates the Divine Hermit before him.

Besides all this, there is neither any purely mundane view whatsoever that does not necessitate some reining of passion and appetite, or that gives them free head and rope altogether. To rein and suppress the passion is an obligation according to every opinion, in the view of every reasoning man, and according to every religion. Therefore let the reasoning man observe these ideals with the eye of his reason, and keep them before his attention and in his mind ; and even if he should not achieve the highest rank and level of this order described in the present book, let him at least cling hold of the meanest level. That is the view of those who advocate the reining of the passion to the extent that will not involve mundane loss in this present life ; for if he tastes some bitterness and unpleasantness at the beginning of his career through reining and suppressing his passion, this will presently be followed by a consequent sweetness and a pleasure in which he may rejoice with great joy and gladness ; while the labour he endures in wrestling with his passion and suppressing his appetites will grow easier by habit, especially if this be effected gradually—by accustoming himself to the discipline and leading on his soul gently, first to deny trifling appetites and to forgo a little of its desires at the requirement of reason and judgment, and then to seek after further discipline until it becomes associated with his character and habit. In this way his appetitive soul will become submissive and will grow accustomed to being subject to his rational soul. So the process will continue to develop ; and the discipline will be reinforced by the joy he has in the results yielded by this

reining of his passion, and the profit he has of his judgment
and reason and of controlling his affairs by them ; by the praise
men lavish upon him, and their evident desire to emulate his
achievement.

CHAPTER III

Summary Prolegomena to the Detailed Account of Each of the Evil Dispositions of the Soul

Now that we have laid level the foundations for that part of our discourse which is to follow, and have mentioned the most important principles as constituting an adequate capital and reserve on which to draw, we will proceed to describe the various evil dispositions of the soul, and the gentle means of reforming them, to serve as an analogy and an example for what we have not attempted to set forth. We shall withal endeavour to be as brief and concise as possible in speaking of these vices ; for we have already established the chief cause and principal reason, from which we shall derive and on which we shall build all the divers treatments necessary for the reformation of any particular evil characteristic. Indeed, if we should not single out even one of these for special consideration, but leave them all aside without any individual mention, ample resources would be available for putting them to right by keeping in mind and holding fast to our first principle. For all these dispositions are the result of obeying the call of passion and yielding to the persuasion of the appetite : to rein and guard these twain will effectively prevent being seized and moulded by them. But in any case we intend to state as much on this subject as we consider needful and necessary to assist in fulfilling the purpose of our present book. And God be our help in this.

CHAPTER IV

Of How a Man may Discover his Own Vices

INASMUCH as it is impossible for any of us to deny his passion, because of the affection he has for his own self and the approval and admiration he feels for his own actions, or to look upon his own character and way of life with the pure and single eye of reason, it can scarcely fall to any man to have a clear view of his vices and reprehensible habits. Since the knowledge of this is denied him, he will hardly depart out of any vice, seeing that he is not even aware of it ; much less will he think it disgraceful and endeavour to be rid of it.

He must therefore rely in this matter upon an intelligent man who is his frequent associate and constant companion. He will ask and implore and insist upon his informing him of whatever he knows of his vices, making him understand that in that way he will be doing what he most desires and what will have the greatest effect on him. He will tell him that he is immensely obliged and infinitely grateful to him for such a kindness. He will beg him not to be shy of him, or blandish him, and will tell him bluntly that if he is easy on him, or dilatory in informing him of anything, he will have done him an injury and deceived him, and will deserve his severe reproaches.

When his supervisor begins to inform him, and to tell him what he sees and discovers about him, he must not exhibit any sorrow or sense of disgrace ; on the contrary he must appear to rejoice at what he hears and to be eager for more. If he observes

36

in any circumstance that his friend has concealed anything from him out of shyness, or has been too moderate in expressing his disapproval, above all if he has actually approved of his conduct, then he will reproach him and make it plain that he is very much upset by him ; he will inform him that he does not like him to act in that way, and that all he desires is perfect frankness and absolute candour. If on the other hand he finds that his mentor has gone too far, and has been excessive in his disapproval and abhorrence at some act of his, he will not therefore fly into a rage ; rather will he applaud him and make him see how happy and pleased he is with his conduct.

Moreover he must renew his request to such a supervisor time and time again ; for evil characteristics and habits have a way of returning after they have been expelled. He should also try to discover and be on the lookout for what his neighbours and colleagues and associates say about him ; what they find to praise in him, and what to blame.

When a man follows this course in these matters, scarcely one of his vices will be hidden from him, however insignificant and secret it may be. Then if it should happen that he falls in with an enemy or an adversary that delights in exposing his weaknesses and vices, he will not have to wait to make good his knowledge of his faults at his hand ; rather he will be compelled and obliged to get rid of them betimes, if he has some regard for himself and is ambitious to be a decent and virtuous man. Galen wrote a book on this subject entitled *Good Men Profit by their Enemies,* in which he gave an account of the benefits he derived from having an enemy ; and another treatise called *How a Man May Discover his Own Vices,* which we have here abstracted and epitomized. What we have set out in this chapter is amply sufficient ; if any man will make use of it, he will ever be like a poised and whetted arrow.

CHAPTER V

Of Carnal Love and Familiarity, with a Summary Account of Pleasure

THE aforesaid men of lofty purpose and soul are far removed from this calamity by their very nature and temperament. For there is nothing more grievous to them than to be mean and humble and abject, to manifest want and need, and to endure injury and arrogance. Having reflected on what lovers must perforce suffer in these respects, they run away from love, holding themselves steadfast, and stopping their passion for love if they are ever afflicted by it. So too do those who are involved in pressing and extreme worldly or other-worldly occupations and cares. But men that are effeminate, flirtatious, idle, soft, and given over to appetite, who make pleasure their sole interest and seek only for worldly gratification, who take it to be a great loss and sorrow to lose it, and reckon what they cannot attain to be a real misery and misfortune—such men are hardly delivered from this affliction. Especially is this the case if they are much addicted to reading lovers' tales, to the recitation of delicate, amorous poetry and to listening to sorrowful music and singing.

Let us now speak of how to be on one's guard against this disposition, and to be awake to its stealthy hidy-holes and lurking-places, so much as befits the object of our present book. And first we will prefix some profitable remarks which will be of help in attaining both what has gone before and what lies ahead in this book; namely, the discussion of Pleasure.

Pleasure consists simply of the restoration of that condition which was expelled by the element of pain, while passing from one's actual state until one returns to the state formerly experienced. An example is provided by the man who leaves a restful, shady spot to go out into the desert ; there he proceeds under the summer sun until he is affected by the heat ; then he returns to his former place. He continues to feel pleasure in that place, until his body returns to its original state ; then he loses the sense of pleasure as his body goes back to normal. The intensity of his pleasure on coming home is in proportion to the degree of intensity of the heat, and the speed of his cooling-off in that place. Hence the philosophers have defined pleasure as a return to the state of nature.

Now since pain and the departure from the state of nature sometimes occur little by little over a long period of time, and then the return to the state of nature happens all at once, in a brief space, under such circumstances we are not aware of the element of pain, whereas the sharpness of the sense of a return to nature is multiplied. This state we call pleasure. Those who have had no training suppose this has happened without any prior pain ; they imagine it as a pure and solitary phenomenon, wholly disassociated from pain. Now this is not really the case at all ; there cannot in fact be any pleasure except in proportion to a prior pain, that of departing from the state of nature. One takes pleasure in eating and drinking according to the degree to which one has hungered and thirsted ; when the hungry and thirsty man returns to his original state, there is no more exquisite torture than to compel him to go on partaking of food and drink, in spite of the fact that just previously he could think of nothing more pleasurable and desirable than these. It is the same with all other pleasures : the definition is universally valid and all-embracing. Nevertheless in order to make this clear we need to discuss the question in more detail, with greater delicacy, and at fuller length than hitherto. We have in fact explained the matter in our book *On the Nature of Pleasure*,[1] and therefore what we have mentioned here will have to suffice for our present needs.

Most of those who incline after pleasure and follow it blindly do not know it for what it really is, and have never imagined it save in the second state—that is, the period extending from the beginning of the end of the painful reaction up to the complete return to the original state. They therefore love pleasure, and desire never under any circumstances to be without it ; not realizing that this is impossible, seeing that it is a state which cannot exist and cannot be known except the original state precede it.

Now the pleasure imagined by lovers and others possessed and infatuated by some passion—such as those in love with authority, rulership, and all other excessive objects infatuation with which dominates some men's souls so that they desire nothing else but to achieve that, and think life worthless without it—this pleasure, I say, seems to them very great indeed and beyond all reckoning when they imagine the realization of their desire. This is because they only imagine the achievement and attaining of their quest—which is a subject very precious to their souls—without it ever occurring to their minds that their original state is so to speak the road and pathway to the attainment of the quest. If they only thought and reflected upon the hardness, roughness and difficulty of that road, upon its dangers and perils and pitfalls, what now seems to them so sweet would appear bitter, and what they make little of would seem very great, by the side of what they have to suffer and endure.

[1] Only fragments in quotation of this work have survived, see P. Kraus, *op. cit.*, pp. 139-64.

Having given the gist of the *Nature of Pleasure* and made clear wherein lie the errors of those who imagine it to be pure and free of suffering and pain, we will now return to our discussion and call attention to the evil qualities of this disposition—love—and its essential baseness.

Lovers transgress the bounds of the animals in their lack of self-control, their failure to rein their passion, and their subservience to their lusts. For they are not content merely with gratifying this lust—that is, sexual enjoyment—in spite of the fact that of all the appetites it is the foulest and the most disreputable in the view of the rational soul that is the true man. They are not content with gratifying it with any means at their disposal, but must needs enjoy it in a particular and precise situation, so that they join and pile up one lust upon another ; they serve and submit to their passion over and over again, and add one slavery to another.   No wild animal goes any way near to this extent in regard to this especial matter ; on the contrary, the beasts gratify their urge to the amount required by nature to get rid of that sensation of suffering and pain which urges them in that direction—so much and no more ; then they recover complete repose from it.   Now since such men do not confine themselves to the animal degree of subservience to instinct, but even invoke the aid of the intellect—which God gave them to mark their superiority over the beasts, and in order that they might see the evil qualities of passion and therefore rein and rule it—so as to scale the most subtle and secret lusts and enjoy them to the last degree of refinement ; it is therefore right and proper that they should never reach any goal or achieve any repose, but forever continue to have the discomfort of a multitude of urges, and to regret the vast amount they miss.   They are never joyous and satisfied by what they have in fact attained and been able to get, because they are always turning away from these lusts and attaching their ambitions to an infinite succession of yet higher pleasures.

Furthermore lovers, because of their obedience to passion and their preference and worship of pleasure, experience sorrow where they precisely suppose that they will rejoice, and pain where they think they will have pleasure. This is because they never reach or attain any single pleasure without being affected and controlled by a sense of anxiety and effort. It may well happen that they will continue in a state of constant anguish and unremitting agony without accomplishing any desire whatsoever. Many of them are reduced by prolonged insomnia, worry and undernourishment to a state of madness and delusion, of consumption and wasting away. Behold them then in the trap and toils of pleasure, dragged down to the most dreadful and horrid fate ! See how the consequences of such " pleasure " have brought them to the extremes of misery and ruin ! As for those who think they will achieve the pleasure of love completely by possessing and having power over it, they have made a palpable mistake and error. For pleasure, when it is attained, is in strict proportion to the degree of suffering and pain that stimulate and incite to such pleasure ; and when a man possesses and has power over anything, the stimulus within him weakens and quietens down and comes to rest rapidly. It is a very true saying that that which is attained is soon wearied of, while that which is denied is mightily desired.

Moreover to part from the beloved is an inescapable necessity, that is to say at death, even if one be secure from all the other mundane accidents and incidents that scatter friends and divide lovers. Since therefore there is no escape from swallowing this anguish and tasting this bitterness, to put it forward and so have rest from it is more expedient than to postpone it and wait for it to happen. For when the inevitable is put forward, one is relieved of the burden of dreading it during the period of its postponement. Besides this, it is obviously simpler and easier to deny the soul its beloved, before love becomes firmly established and dominant over the soul. Once familiarity is added to affection, it is much more difficult to break away and get free of it. For the bane of familiarity is no whit less than the bane of love ; indeed, it would not be wrong to say that it is even stronger and further-reaching.

When the duration of love is short, and the meetings with the beloved are few, it is more likely that love will not be confounded and fortified with familiarity. The judgment of reason therefore decrees on this consideration too that one should act betimes in denying the soul and reining it from love before it ever falls into love, or to wean it from love if it should succumb to it before its love becomes firmly established. This is the argument which Plato used in the case of a pupil who was afflicted by an attachment for a girl and therefore failed to be in his place in Plato's classes. He ordered that the student should be sought and brought before him. When he appeared, he said, " Tell me, friend—do you doubt that some day you will have to part from this girl friend of yours ? " " I do not doubt that," the young man answered. " Well then," said Plato, " let yourself taste to-day the bitterness which you must certainly swallow on that day, and make yourself rid of the intervening constant dread of anticipation—the anticipation of what must inevitably come to pass—and the difficulty of dealing with that emotion after it has taken firm hold of you and has been further reinforced by familiarity." It is said that the pupil replied to Plato, " Wise Master, what you say is true. But I feel that my anticipation of that event will become a consolation with the passage of time, and will become lighter for me to bear." Plato retorted, " How can you have confidence in the consolation of

D

time, and not fear the familiarity it brings ? Why are you so
sure that the circumstances of parting will not come upon you
before you are consoled, and yet after your love is firmly established ? In that case your anguish would be heightened and
your bitterness redoubled." It is related that the youth pros-
trated himself before Plato in that same hour, expressing his
gratitude to him with praise and blessings ; he neither returned
to his former state, nor exhibited any sorrow or longing, and
from that time forward he continued in attendance at Plato's
classes without ever failing. It is added that after this discourse
Plato turned to his, other pupils and upbraided them for leaving
the youth to his own devices and allowing him to devote his
energies to the other branches of philosophy before he had
reformed and suppressed his appetitive soul and subjected it to
his rational soul.

Now because certain silly people contend and wage war with
the philosophers about this conception, using language as weak
and flaccid as themselves—and they forsooth called wits and
literary gentlemen—we propose to set down what they have to
say on the subject and then give our own version of it.

They say that love is a habit only of refined natures and subtle
brains, and that it encourages cleanliness, elegance, spruceness
and a handsome turn-out. They accompany such statements
by quoting eloquent lyrics to the same effect, and fortify their
argument with references to men of letters, poets, chiefs and
leaders who indulged in love, even going so far as to include
prophets. To this we answer that refinement of nature and
mental subtlety and clarity are recognized and proven by the
capacity of those so endowed to comprehend obscure, remote
matters and fine, subtle sciences, to express clearly difficult and
complicated ideas, and to invent useful and profitable arts.
Now these things we find only in the philosophers ; whereas we

observe that love-making is not their habit, but the frequent and constant use of Bedouins, Kurds, Nabateans [1] and such-like clodhoppers. We also discover it to be a general and universal fact that there is no nation on earth of finer intellect and more evident wisdom than the Greeks, who on the whole are less preoccupied by love than any other people.

This proves the very opposite of what the others claim ; that is to say, it proves that love is in fact the habit of gross natures and stupid minds ; for those who are little given to thought, reflection and deliberation run headlong after the call of their natures and the inclination of their appetites. As for their argument about the great number of literary men, poets, chiefs and leaders who have indulged in love, to this we answer that headship and leadership, poetry and purity of speech are not the invariable and indisputable signs of perfect intelligence and wisdom. This being so, it is entirely possible that men of the kind described who have been great lovers were in reality quite deficient in intelligence and wisdom. But those who argue against us are so ignorant and silly that they suppose knowledge and wisdom to consist solely of grammar, poetry, correctness of speech and eloquence ; they are quite unaware that philosophers do not count a single one of these subjects as wisdom, or those skilled in them as wise. On the contrary, their idea of a wise man is he who knows the conventions and rules of logical demonstration, and succeeds to acquire and achieve the highest degree of mathematical, physical and metaphysical knowledge that lies within human capacity.

I remember once being present when one of these smart fellows was engaged with a shaikh of ours at Baghdad ; the aforesaid shaikh, besides being a philosopher, had considerable competence in grammar, lexicography and poetry. The

[1] A term applied contemptuously to certain peasants.

fellow argued with him and bandied quotations against him, jeering and sneering all the while he spoke, going to great lengths of exaggerated encomium in praise of those who practised his particular art, while he vilified all other men. The whole time the shaikh bore with him, well knowing his ignorance and conceit, the while he smiled at me. Finally the fellow exclaimed, " This is in fact what science really is ; all the rest is mere wind." Then the shaikh said, " My son, that is the science of the man who has no real knowledge ; it rejoices those who are without intellect." Turning to me, he prompted me, " Ask this lad here some questions relating to the elements of the ' necessary ' sciences. He is one of those who think that they who are skilled in lexicography can answer any enquiry that is put to them." I said, " Tell me about the sciences—are they necessary or conventional ? " I did not complete the division on purpose ; but he at once blurted out, " All the sciences are conventional." This was because he had heard one of our companions reproaching this group on the grounds that their science was conventional, and so he wanted to criticize them in the same terms, not being aware of what they had further on this subject. Then I asked him, " Take the case of the man who knows that the moon will be eclipsed on such-and-such a night, and that scammony [1] liberates the stomach when it is seized, or that litharge neutralizes the acidity of vinegar when it is pounded and thrown into it—is his knowledge of this correct only because people conventionally adopt these opinions ? " " No," he answered. " Then whence did he derive his knowledge ? " I went on. Now he lacked the discrimination to see whither I was leading him ; and so he said, " I say that all sciences are necessary, supposing that it

[1] " A cathartic gum-resin obtained from a species of convolvulus in Asia Minor " (*Chambers's Twentieth Century Dictionary*).

was permissible to include in this category grammar." "Very well then," I proceeded. "Tell me about the man who knows that the simple vocative is put in the nominative whereas the compound vocative is put in the accusative [1]—is his knowledge of something necessary and natural, or is it of something conventional according to the general consensus of opinion?" He stammered out something he had heard from his professors, trying to prove that this was a necessary matter ; while I proceeded to show him how he had contradicted himself and how his argument fell to pieces, which reduced him to a state of shame and great confusion and dismay. Then the shaikh began to laugh at him, saying, "My son, try the taste of a science that really is a science !"

We have only recounted this story in order that it may serve as an additional encouragement and incentive to the nobler part ; for that is the sole object we have before us in this book. It is far from our intention, where we have sought to demonstrate ignorance and deficiency in the course of our present discussion, to condemn all who have concerned themselves with grammar and linguistics or have made these their occupation and study ; for some of these scholars have been additionally blessed by God with an ample portion of the true sciences. Our purpose is merely to expose those ignoramuses who think that no other science exists but these two, and that these alone qualify a man to be called learned.

It remains for us to deal with an argument about which we have not yet said anything, namely their attempt to exonerate carnal love on the grounds that even the prophets were afflicted by it. Now there is surely nobody who is prepared to allow that love-making should be accounted one of the merits or virtues of the prophets, or that it is something they particularly

[1] Rhazes refers to a rule of Arabic grammar.

chose and approved ; on the contrary, it is to be reckoned among
their slips and peccadilloes.   This being so, there are no grounds
whatsoever for exonerating or embellishing or applauding or
propagating love on account of the prophets.   For it behoves
us to incite and urge ourselves to emulate those actions of
virtuous men which they found pleasing and approved in themselves and desired that others should imitate, not those slips and
peccadilloes which they regretted and of which they repented,
wishing they had never happened to them or been committed
by them.

As for their assertion that love encourages cleanliness, elegance, a handsome turn-out and spruceness : what is the use of
a beautiful physique, when the soul is ugly ?   Who wants
physical beauty anyway, or labours to attain it, except women
and effeminates ?   It is recorded that a certain man invited a
philosopher to his house ; all its appointments were extremely
fine and splendid, but the man himself was excessively ignorant
and stupid and idiotic.   The philosopher examined attentively
everything in the house, and then spat at the man himself.
When the fellow burst into a fit of anger, the philosopher said,
" Do not be angry.   I looked at everything in your house with
the greatest care, but I saw nothing fouler or filthier than yourself ; so as I thought you were very suitable for the purpose, I
made you my spittoon."   It is said that thereafter the man took
a humble opinion of his situation and became eager for learning
and speculation.

Since we have already mentioned before the subject of
familiarity, we will now discourse a little on its nature, and how
to be on one's guard against it.   Familiarity is an accident that
befalls the soul as a result of long companionship, coupled with
a reluctance to be parted from the person so accompanied ; it
too is a vast affliction that increases and augments with the

passage of time, and yet is not sensed until the actual moment of parting, when it suddenly bursts forth all at once in a most painful form, exceedingly distressing to the soul. This disposition affects the beasts as well, though in some it is more marked than in others. The method of guarding against it is constantly to dispose oneself to parting from one's companion, never forgetting this and never losing heed of it, but to train oneself gradually to practise it.

We have now set out what is sufficient for this chapter ; we will therefore proceed to speak of conceit.

CHAPTER VI

Of Conceit

BECAUSE every man is in love with himself, his admiration of every fine quality he possesses is of necessity above its merits, while his disapprobation of every bad quality is correspondingly below its deserts. Whereas on the other hand his admiration of the good and disapprobation of the bad in others are exactly just, if they be free of love or hate ; for then his reason is clear, and unclouded and uninfluenced by passion. It is on this account that if a man has the least virtue, it becomes enormous in his eyes and he is eager to be applauded for it above his due ; and when this state of mind gets a firm hold on him it converts into conceit ; especially if he find others to assist him in this by encouraging and applauding him as much as he desires.

Now one of the calamities of conceit is that it leads to the diminution of the very thing about which a man originally became conceited ; for a conceited man never seeks to increase or improve, or acquire from others, the quality about which he is conceited. A man who is conceited about his horse does not seek to exchange it for one that is still brisker, for he thinks that no horse can possibly be brisker than his ; similarly a man who is conceited about his work will never try to improve it, because he thinks that it cannot be improved. And when a man ceases to desire more of anything, it inevitably diminishes and he falls away from the level of his rivals and equals ; for the latter, if they be not conceited, continue to seek improvement and therefore go on improving and progressing until soon they surpass the conceited man while he finds himself left behind.

A method of repelling conceit is to entrust the estimate of one's bad and good qualities to another, in the manner we have described when we were discussing how a man may discover his own vices. He should not estimate or judge himself in reference to people who are mean and worthless and who have not an abundance of the quality about which he is conceited, or live in a town whose inhabitants are of this sort. If a man is on his guard in these two respects, he will find every day something occurring to him that will incline him to underestimate himself rather than to be conceited. In short, he should not begin to have a good opinion of himself until he has surpassed all his rivals in the judgment of others ; nor to have a mean opinion of himself until he falls below them and those inferior to him and them in other men's eyes. If he does this, and keeps himself straight in this way, he will be innocent of vain conceit and base meanness, and people will call him a man who knows his own worth.

What we have mentioned is sufficient for this chapter ; we will therefore proceed to speak of envy.

CHAPTER VII

Of Envy

ENVY is another evil disposition, springing from a combination in the soul of miserliness and greed. Those who discourse upon the reformation of character call a man malicious when he takes pleasure instinctively in injuries that befall others while resenting anything that occurs to their advantage, even though they never injured or offended him in any way. Similarly they give the name of benevolent to the man who is glad and takes pleasure in whatever occurs to the advantage and profit of others. Envy is worse than miserliness, because the miser merely does not want and does not think to give anyone anything that belongs to him or is his property ; whereas the envious man does not want anyone to obtain anything good whatsoever, even though it be something he does not himself own. Envy is indeed a grievously hurtful disease of the soul.

A method of repelling it is for the intelligent man to examine envy, for he will find that it has a large share of the stamp of malice ; the envious man is stamped as resenting what happens to the advantage of those who never injured or offended him. This is one half of the definition of malice ; and the malicious man deserves the hatred both of God and men—of God, because his will is diametrically opposed to God's, seeing that God is the All-Bountiful and desires the good of all men ; and of men, because he is hateful and unjust to mankind. For whoever wishes evil to befall any man whatsoever, and does not wish good to come to him, is thereby proven hateful to him ; and if that man has further never injured or offended him, then he is unjust to him into the bargain. Furthermore, the person envied has never deprived the envier of any of his possessions, or prevented him from achieving anything that he might have gained, or used him in any way to his own advantage. This being so, he, the envied, is in exactly the same position as any other man who has obtained some good and realized his hopes, and whom the envier has never seen at all. How then should he not envy those living in India and China? If he does not envy them because he has never seen them, it is only necessary for him to picture them as they are, living in the lap of luxury. Now if it be folly and madness to grieve over what they have obtained, and the hopes they have realized, it is equally foolish and mad to grieve and sorrow over what those who are actually before him have obtained, since they are in the same position as those who are absent from him in the sense that they never robbed him of anything he possessed or prevented him from achieving anything he might have gained or used him in any way to their own advantage. There is not the slightest difference between those whom the envier can see and those he cannot, except the actual fact of his being able to contemplate their circumstances, the very like of which he may readily imagine in the case of those who are absent from him, and know and be quite sure that they are enjoying precisely the same advantages.

Some men err in their definition of envy, so much so that they label as envious those who only resent good happening to people whose success involves them in some injury and trouble. . Yet it is not proper to call anyone of that kind envious ; rather the term ought to be applied absolutely to those who are upset when another man obtains something good where they experience no injury whatsoever ; while the excessively envious man is similarly upset even when there is something to his advantage in the other man's good fortune. When injuries and troubles result, they have the effect of creating not envy but a corresponding enmity in the soul.

This sort of mutual envy only arises practically speaking as between relatives, associates and acquaintances. Thus we may observe that when a stranger rules over a community, the people of that province scarcely discover any resentment of the fact within themselves ; then if one of their own townsfolk comes to power, hardly a single man escapes from a sense of resentment, despite the fact that the townsman may be far more considerate and compassionate towards them than the stranger. People are brought to this pass by their extreme self-love ; each one of them, because of this love for himself, wishes to be the first to reach the coveted offices rather than anyone else. So, when they see someone outstripping them and advanced over them who was but yesterday at their own level, they are very much upset and find it very hard and irksome to stomach his out-stripping them. They are not in the least gratified by his sympathy and kindness towards them ; their hearts are still firmly attached to the ambition of achieving what the other has beaten them to, and nothing else will content or mollify them. As for the stranger who comes to rule them, since they never saw him in his former state they do not picture how completely he has outstripped and surpassed them, and therefore they feel less grief and regret. In such circumstances it is necessary to have recourse to reason, and to reflect on what I am about to say on this subject.

There are no grounds whatever in justice for the envious man's rage and fury and hatred of the neighbour who has out-stripped him. He has never prevented his rival from competing with him to reach the goal, even though it was he who achieved and attained it instead of the other. The fortune which the successful man obtained is not something the envier had a better right to or a greater need of. Then let him not hate or be furious with him ; let him keep his fury rather for himself, or for his luck perhaps or his slackness—for it was one or the other of these that deprived and disqualified him from achieving his ambition. Moreover if the successful one is his brother or cousin, or a kinsman or acquaintance or townsman, his success is to the greater advantage of the envier, encouraging the hope that he will secure his welfare and giving him greater protection against his malice ; for there is between them the bond of relationship, which is a strong and natural tie. Further, since there must of necessity be some men that are the chiefs and kings, wealthy and of great possessions, while the envier neither expects nor hopes that what they have will pass to him or to anyone whose proprietorship will be to his profit, there are no grounds whatever in reason for him to resent the other's continued enjoyment of his possessions, since it is all one to him whether he is the owner or someone else whose ownership is equally unprofitable to him.

Again we say that the reasonable man will rein his animal soul by means of the perspicacity of his rational soul and the strength of his choleric soul, so as to restrain it from enjoying even the things that are pleasurable and delicious, let alone that which is neither appetizing nor pleasing and is at the same time positively harmful to both soul and body. I would add that envy is one of those things in which there is no pleasure ; or even if it contains some degree of pleasure, it is very much less than all other pleasures ; it is moreover harmful to both soul and body. It harms the soul, because it is a stupefying influence, robbing the soul of its powers of reflection and so preoccupying it that it is not free to control even the things that profit the body and itself, because of the evil dispositions, such as prolonged sorrow, anxiety and care, that affect the soul in association with it. It harms the body, because when these accidents befall the soul, the body is exposed to prolonged insomnia and malnutrition, and these bring in their train a poor colour, a muddy complexion and a disordered temperament. When the reasonable man reins his passion by means of his reason—for passion commends to him pleasurable appetites though they have previously been followed by discomfort—it is all the more proper for him to strive to expunge this disposition from his soul, to forget and forsake it, and to cease thinking about it whenever it occurs to his mind.

There is the additional point that envy is an admirable ally assisting the envied to take revenge upon the envier. For envy keeps the envier perpetually anxious ; it fuddles his mind and tortures the body ; by preoccupying his soul and weakening his body it enfeebles his cunning and endeavours against the envied if it continues long enough. What judgment then is more deserving of condemnation and contempt than that which brings only harm upon those who adopt it ? What weapon is better fit to be cast away than that which protects the enemy while wounding him that bears it ?

Another method of expunging envy from the soul and making it easier and pleasanter to give it up is for the intelligent man to consider the conditions of various men during their progress upwards, and while they are reaching their cherished goal, and their circumstances when they have finally achieved what they sought in these ways. If he will ponder this carefully in the light of our present remarks, he will discover that the inward state of the envied man is quite the opposite of what his envier supposes ; the picture which the latter draws of the former, in all his grandeur and splendour, his extreme happiness and enjoyment, is quite untrue. Let me add that men never cease admiring and wondering at a given state, wishing and longing to achieve and attain it, and thinking that those who have reached it and attained it are without a doubt in the last degree of beatitude and gratification. But when they themselves reach and attain that state, their joy and happiness last for a very brief time, no longer in fact than the time required for them to be fixed and established in that state and to be known to have achieved it. During this short period a man considers himself really fortunate and happy. But when the yearned-for state is actually realized, when he is firmly established in his possession of it and is known by others to be so situated, his soul yearns for greater heights and his hopes are fixed on yet loftier reaches. So he comes to belittle and despise his hard-won circumstances, that were previously his entire goal and ambition. Then he finds himself torn between anxiety and fear—fear lest he should lose the advancement he has already succeeded in winning, and anxiety to achieve what he reckons still to attain. So he is perpetually desperate, dissatisfied and disappointed with his existing circumstances ; he wears out his thoughts and his body inventing means to shift out of that level and climb up still higher. Yet his second state is still the same, and he feels no different when he reaches a third level and attains any other state.

This being so, it behoves the intelligent man not to envy any of his fellows on account of some superfluity of worldly goods which the other may have obtained and which he can very well do without and yet maintain a reasonable level of subsistence ; he should not suppose that those who have greater and ampler means enjoy a superior ease and pleasure corresponding with their more abundant worldly wealth. For such men, by reason of the long continuance and constancy of those circumstances, after first enjoying prolonged ease and leisure come in the end not to enjoy their advantages at all, because they are finally regarded by them as something quite natural, and necessary to keep them alive ; and so their enjoyment tends to approximate to the enjoyment any man experiences in his habitual circumstances. Such too is the case as regards lack of repose ; since they are always striving and struggling to improve themselves and to climb up still higher, they get little rest, perhaps even less than those inferior to them in circumstance ; I would go further, and say that in the majority of cases that is in fact always and invariably true.

When the intelligent man regards these facts considerately, using his reason while doing so and putting aside his passion, he will realize that the utmost attainable limit of a pleasant and reposeful life is summed up in a modest competence. Whatever goes beyond that in the circumstances of living is pretty much of a muchness ; in fact, competence always furnishes the superior ease. What reason therefore remains to justify mutual envy, except it be ignorance of these things, and a disposition to follow the dictates of passion rather than reason ?

What we have now mentioned is sufficient for this chapter ; we will therefore proceed to speak of anger.

CHAPTER VIII

Of Repelling Anger

ANGER is put into an animal to be a means of taking revenge upon another that causes it pain. When this disposition is taken to excess and surpasses its proper bounds, to the extent that reason is lost in consequence, it may well be that the injury and suffering it brings upon the one moved by this emotion will prove severer and more grievous than that endured by the object of such anger. It therefore behoves the intelligent man to recall frequently the cases of those whom anger has brought sooner or later to disagreeable circumstances, and to try to picture himself in their predicament when his anger is roused. For many men when they are angry are apt to strike out with their fists and slap and even butt with their heads, and often enough hurt themselves more than the person with whom they are angry. I have seen a man punch another on the jaw and dislocate his fingers in doing so, so that he had to nurse them for a long time, whereas his victim came to no great harm. I once saw another man get into a rage and scream and spit blood on the spot ; that led on to consumption, which caused his death. We have heard tell of men who during the time of their anger have brought suffering upon their families and children and dear ones for which they repented a long while, and which they perhaps never put right till the end of their lives. Galen states that his mother used to rush at a padlock with her mouth and bite it if it was difficult for her to open. Upon my life, there is no great difference between the man who loses his powers of thought and reflection when he is angry and a lunatic.

If a man will constantly keep such situations in mind while he is normal, he is more likely to be able to picture them when anger seizes him. He should be aware that those who do such monstrous things when they are angry are only brought to that pass because they lose their reason at that time ; and so he ought to see to it that when he is angry he will not do anything except after due thought and deliberation, lest he injure himself where he intended to injure another. He should not share with the beasts in liberating action without reflection. And during the time he is inflicting punishment, he ought to be free of four emotions—arrogance, anger against the person he is punishing, and the opposites of these two ; for the two former states of mind provoke him to make his punishment and vengeance exceed the dimension of the crime, while the two latter result in their being too lenient. If the intelligent man will keep these ideas in mind, and prevail upon his passion to follow them out, his anger and revenge will be proportionately just, and he will be secure from suffering any consequent injury to his soul or body in this world or the next.

CHAPTER IX

Of Casting Away Mendacity

THIS is another evil disposition which is due to the provocation of passion. When a man loves authority and domination in whatever form and under whatever circumstance, he wants always to be the one to teach and give information, because that gives him an advantage over the recipient of such tidings. Now we have already remarked that the intelligent man ought not to liberate his passion when he fears that this may afterwards involve him in worry, pain and regret ; and we find that lying involves the liar in precisely these consequences. For the chronic and habitual liar is bound to be exposed ; he can hardly escape it, either because he contradicts himself through carelessness or bad memory, or because someone he is talking to knows that the facts are contrary to what he states. The liar can never obtain anything near so much pleasure and enjoyment in lying, though he should lie all his life, much less equal, the worry and disgrace and shame at being exposed, even on one occasion in the whole of his career, and despised and held up to the ridicule and contempt and disapprobation of his fellows, who are likely to be little inclined to rely on him and trust him thereafter ; provided of course he has some self-respect, and is not utterly base and abandoned. But such a creature as the latter ought not to be reckoned as a man, much less be made the object of discourse aimed at his reformation.

Because the means of exposure in this matter may sometimes be very late in coming, the ignorant man is liable to be led astray in this ; but the intelligent man does not plunge himself into a course when he fears (or does not feel secure against) its involving him in disgraceful exposure ; rather does he make his dispositions and resolve himself prudently to avoid that.

There are two varieties, as I see it, of untruthful information. In one kind the informant has in view some seemly and commendable object which will clearly excuse him when the facts are discovered and prove to the advantage of the person informed, obliging him to tell the story in the way he has even though there is no truth in it. For example, if a man knows that a certain ruler is resolved upon executing a friend of his upon the morrow, but that when the morrow is over the ruler will come into possession of certain facts obliging him not to kill his friend. If therefore he comes to his friend and tells him that he has hidden some treasure in his house, and requires his assistance the following day ; if he then takes him home with him and keeps him busy there all that day, plying him to dig and search for the treasure, until the day is past and the king comes into possession of the said facts, and he then tells his friend the whole truth of the matter—I say that that man, even though in the first place he tells his friend what is entirely untrue, is nevertheless not to be blamed, neither is he exposed to shame when the facts are discovered to be contrary to his account of them, since his object was seemly and respectable, and of advantage to the person receiving the information. Such examples of untruthful information as these involve the informant in no disgrace or blame or regret ; on the contrary, they bring him gratitude and seemly approbation.

As for the second variety which lacks this commendable purpose, there discovery certainly means disgrace and blame—disgrace, if the person informed suffers no harm whatsoever, as for example when a man tells his friend that he has seen in such-and-such a city a certain animal or precious stone or plant of such-and-such a kind and description, and there is no truth at all in what he says, the liar's object being merely to provoke admiration in the other ; or blame, if his information brings harm to his informant into the bargain, as for instance when a man tells his friend that the ruler of a remote land desires and yearns for his company, and he is confident within himself that if he takes horse and proceeds thither he will secure from him a certain place and rank, but he only acts as he does in order to get possession of something the other leaves behind, and then, his friend having taken the trouble to ride off and come at great labour to that ruler's court, he discovers that there is not an atom of truth in the whole story, and finds to boot that the ruler is angry and enraged against him, and he is ruined.

All the same it is better to call a man a liar, and to avoid and beware of him, if he lies not out of necessity nor with any important object in view ; for if a man approves of lying and indulges in it for mean and worthless ends, it is all the more likely and probable that he will do so when he has large and important advantages in view.

CHAPTER X

Of Miserliness

THIS disposition cannot be described as wholly due to passion. For we find some people are prompted to be tight-fisted and careful with their possessions by excessive fear of poverty and a far-sighted consideration of the consequences, as well as an extreme caution in taking measures against misfortunes and hardships. Others on the contrary take pleasure in keeping things to themselves purely for its own sake. Thus we may observe how some boys are entirely lacking in thought and prudence, and give away all they possess to their playmates, while other boys are quite miserly.

It is therefore necessary to combat this disposition when it springs merely out of passion : this diagnosis is confirmed when one asks a person what reason he has for holding on to his possessions and he cannot find any clear and acceptable argument proving a coherent excuse, but answers in a botchy and patched-up manner with much confusion and repetition. I once asked a tight-fisted man why he behaved in that way, and his response was of the kind I have described. I then proceeded to show him how bad his answer was, and that he had no real reason for being so mean. I did not demand of him that he should give away money in a manner he would notice, much less that he should ruin himself or disburse more than he could readily afford. The end of the matter was that he said to me, " That is what I want, that is how I would like to do." So I made him realize that he had turned aside from the arbitrament of reason to follow his passion, since the excuses he had adopted could not affect either his actual circumstances or his prudence and security and his consideration for the future.

That is the degree of this disposition that requires to be amended, so that passion may not be allowed to consort freely with it : namely, to be miserly over what cannot effect a catastrophic decline in one's present circumstances, or render it difficult or impossible for one to achieve the fortune one aims at attaining. When however a man has a clear and valid excuse on one or other of these grounds, or on both, his canniness is not the result of passion but is due to reason and deliberation, and it ought not to be abolished but increased and confirmed. Still, not every canny person is free to advance the second of these arguments. When a man has despaired, for all his caution, of achieving a higher or more important position than that which he already holds—if for instance he is at the end of his life, or if he has attained the furthest advancement open to his like—in such an event he cannot rest his case at all on the second line of reasoning.

CHAPTER XI

Of Repelling Excessive and Hurtful Anxiety and Worry

THESE two dispositions, although affections of the reason, are nevertheless just as hurtful and deleterious when present in excess, in the way of denying access to the achievement of our desires, as the lack of them, as we have already explained when we discussed the excessive activity of the rational soul. It therefore behoves an intelligent man to give his body repose from them, and to indulge it in as much diversion and amusement and pleasure as it requires to keep it fit and maintain it in good health ; otherwise the body will weaken and become emaciated and finally collapse, so preventing us from reaching our goal.

Because men differ so much in temperament and habit, there is also a difference in the amount of anxiety and worry they can stand ; some can endure a great deal of them without being adversely affected, while others are unable to put up with so much. This power of endurance needs to be looked after and taken care of and gradually increased as much as possible before the matter becomes too difficult ; habit is of great help and assistance here. In short, we ought to indulge in diversion and amusement and pleasure not for their own sakes, but in order that we may be recreated and strengthened to engage the thought and care we require to reach our purpose. As the traveller's object in giving his horse provender is not to give it the pleasure of eating but to strengthen it so that it may bring him safely to his lodging-place, so it is necessary for us to act in watching over the interests of our bodies.

If we act in this way and give the matter this amount of consideration, we shall attain our goals in the quickest time they can possibly be reached ; we shall not be like the man who destroyed his mount before ever coming to the land he intended by over-loading and overstraining it, neither shall we resemble the other man who was so concerned with pampering and fattening his horse that the time went by in which he ought to have reached his stage and lodging-place.

Let us give a further example. Say a man wanted to study philosophy, and was so fond of it that he devoted all his care and occupied all his thought to that one end. Then he had the ambition to rival Socrates, Plato, Aristotle, Theophrastus, Eudemus, Chrysippus, Themistius and Alexander,[1] say in the period of one year. So he prolonged his cogitations and specu-lations, and took less and less food and repose—for insomnia would be the inevitable result of such a procedure. I say that this man would become a prey to delusion and melancholia, consumption and wasting away ere the whole of that time was past, and long before he in any way approached the philosophers we have named. I would add that if another man also desired to attain a perfect knowledge of philosophy, but only looked into it from time to time when he had no other occupation and was bored with his pleasures and appetites, whereas if the slightest task occurred to him or if his least appetite was stirred he at once stopped his studies and returned to his former routine—I repeat that this man would never completely master philosophy in the whole of his life, nor would he come anywhere near to doing so. Both these men would therefore have failed to achieve their purpose ; the one because of excess, the other owing to short-coming. Hence it behoves us to be moderate in our anxieties and worries if we aim at achieving our purposes ; then indeed we will reach our goals, and not fail on account of shortcoming or excess.

[1] Alexander of Aphrodisias. For Rhazes' knowledge of Greek sources, see Introduction, p. 10.

CHAPTER XII

Of Repelling Grief

WHEN the passion through the reason pictures the loss of a beloved associate, grief thereby follows. We need a very long and detailed discussion in order to make clear whether grief is an affection of the reason or the passion ; but we have already stated at the beginning of this book that we shall not here enter into any discussion unless it be unavoidable in view of the purpose we have here been pursuing. On this account we shall leave aside the discussion of this theme and proceed straight to the purpose at which we have aimed in this book. Still, it may be possible for anyone with the slightest grasp of philosophy to deduce and extract this idea from the sketch we have made of grief at the beginning of the discourse. Now we will have done with that and leave it on one side in order to go after our principal purpose.

Since grief clouds the thought and reason, and is harmful alike to soul and body, it is our duty to endeavour to dismiss and repel it, or at any rate to reduce and diminish it as much as possible. This can be done in two different ways. The first is to be on one's guard against it before it actually comes in order that it may not happen, or if it does, so that it will be as slight as possible. The second is to repel and banish it when it has occurred, either wholly or to the greatest possible extent, and to take precautions betimes either in order that it may not happen, or if it does, so that it will be slight and weak. This may be accomplished by reflecting on the ideas which I am now about to mention.

Since the substance out of which sorrows are generated is simply and solely the loss of one's loved ones, and since it is impossible that these loved ones should not be lost because men have their turns with them and by reason of the fact that they are subject to the succession of generation and corruption, it follows that the man most severely afflicted by grief must be he who has the greatest number of loved ones and whose love is the most ardent, while the man least affected by grief is he whose circumstances are the reverse. It would therefore seem that the intelligent man ought to cut away from himself the substance of his griefs, by making himself independent of the things whose loss involves him in grief ; and that he should not be deceived and deluded by the sweetness they impart while they remain in being, but rather keep in mind and image the bitterness that must be tasted when they are lost.

If it be objected that he who takes the precaution of not making and acquiring loved ones, because he is afraid of the grief of losing them, merely hastens forward the day of grief ; the answer would be that even if his precautions and previsions do have this result, the grief such a man hastens forward is by no means equal to that he fears to fall into. A man who has no children cannot be so grief-stricken as the man who loses his child ; this is true even if the childless man is of the sort that grieves because he has no child—I leave out of account those who do not trouble or care or grieve about such a matter at all. The grief of him who has no darling is nothing beside the grief of him who loses his darling.

It is said that someone remarked to a philosopher, " If only you took a child ! " To this the philosopher replied, " The trouble and grief I have trying to keep this body and soul of mine in health tax me beyond my powers—how then should I add and join to them the like again ? " I once heard an intelli-

gent woman remark, " One day I saw a woman terribly dis-
tressed over the loss of a child—so much so that she was afraid
to go near her husband for fear that she might find herself having
another child on whose account she might suffer equal affliction."

Because the possession of the beloved is agreeable and congenial to nature, and the loss thereof is contrary and repugnant
to nature, the soul is bound to be more sensitive to the pain of
losing the beloved than to the pleasure of having him. In the
same way a man may be in good health for a long time and feel
no pleasure in being so, yet if he is affected by sickness in one
of his members he immediately feels severe pain there. So it
is with all loved persons : so long as they are there, or one has
their company for a long while, one ceases to feel such pleasure
in their existence, but as soon as one loses them one is smitten
by severe pain at their loss. It is for this reason that if a man
has enjoyed for a long time the possession of a family and a
precious child, and is then afflicted by the loss of both, he
experiences in a single day, nay, a single hour, a sense of pain
exceeding and obliterating the pleasure he formerly enjoyed in
having them. This is because nature accounts and reckons all
that long enjoyment as her due and right ; nay, she counts it as
yet less than her right, for even in those circumstances she is
never without the feeling that what she possesses is very little,
and is constantly and forevermore wanting to have more of it,
being as she is so fond and avid of pleasure.

This being so—since the pleasure and enjoyment felt in having
loved ones, while they are there, is something so poor, so
obscure, so feeble and inconsiderable, whereas the grief, distress
and anguish of losing them are so palpable, so huge, so painful
and ruinous ; what is one to do, but get rid of them altogether,
or assert one's independence of them, in order that their evil
consequences, their train of hurtful, wasting griefs, may be

destroyed or at least diminished ? This is the highest level that can be reached on this topic, and the most effective in amputating the very substance of grief.

After this it follows that a man should picture and represent to himself the loss of his loved ones, and keep this constantly in his mind and imagination, knowing that it is impossible for them to continue unchanged forever. He should never for a moment give up remembering this and putting it into his thoughts, strengthening his resolve and fortifying his endurance against the day when the calamity happens. That is the way to train and gradually to discipline and strengthen the soul, so that it will protest little when misfortunes occur ; because one has been little habituated and felt small trust and reliance in the survival of the loved ones during the time they were actually there, and one has frequently represented to the soul and inured and familiarized it with the picturing of those misfortunes before they occurred. It was in this sense that the poet said :

> The man of prudence pictures in his soul,
> Ere they descend, what mishaps may befall :
> So, come they sudden, he is not dismayed,
> Having within his soul their image laid.
> He views the matter reaching to its worst,
> And what must hap at last, faces at first.

If however a man is excessively cowardly and extremely inclined to passion and pleasure, and he cannot trust himself to use anything of these twain devices, it is not necessary for him to endeavour to satisfy himself with one beloved out of his many, and to regard her as indispensable and irreplaceable ; he should on the contrary adopt several, so as to have one always to stand in the stead (or come near to doing so) of any he may unfortunately lose. In this way it is possible for his sorrow and grief not to be extreme over the loss of any of them.

This is a summary of the precautions that may be taken against the fact and the occurrence of grief. As for the manner in which grief may be repelled or lessened when it has become a reality and has actually happened, we shall proceed to discourse on that subject now.

When the intelligent man examines and considers those things within this world which are affected by the alternation of generation and corruption, when he perceives that their element is changeable and dissoluble and fluid, that nothing is constant or permanent as an individual, but rather that all things pass away and perish and change and decay and vanish; when he reflects on all this, he ought not to take too much to heart or feel too outraged or stricken by the sudden deprivation of anything. On the contrary, he must reckon the period of their survival to be an advantage, and the enjoyment he has of them a positive gain, seeing that they will inevitably perish and cease to be. Then it will not seem so very terrible or important to him when the end comes, because that is a thing which must come upon them sooner or later. So long as he goes on desiring that they should survive for ever, he is yearning for the impossible, and by yearning for the impossible he is bound to bring grief upon himself, and follow the inclinations of his passion rather than his reason. Moreover the loss of those things that are not necessary to the continuance of life does not call for everlasting grief and sorrow; they are soon replaced and made good, and this leads on to consolation and oblivion; gaiety returns, and things come back to what they were before the misfortune happened. How many men we have seen struck down by a terrible and shocking calamity, and presently pick themselves up again, until they became exactly as they were before the blow fell, enjoying life to the full and entirely content with their circumstances!

It therefore behoves the intelligent man to remind himself, when the misfortune is upon him, how it will presently pass and give way and he will return once more to normality ; he should present this picture to his mind, and stir within himself the desire for its realization, all the time drawing to himself what may preoccupy and divert his thoughts as much as possible, to speed his emergence into this settled state. The impact of grief can also be greatly lightened and assuaged by reminding oneself how many there are that share one's misfortunes, and how scarcely a single man is free of them ; by remembering too how others have been after the blow has fallen, and the various ways they have consoled themselves ; and then by considering his own circumstances and how he has previously consoled himself, when and if misfortunes have come upon him before.

Furthermore, if it be true that the man most severely afflicted by grief is he who has the greatest number of loved ones and whose love is the most ardent, all the same the loss of one of them is bound to result in a corresponding diminution of grief ; indeed such a loss relieves his soul of perpetual worry and anticipatory fear, so that he acquires a wariness and a fortitude to endure subsequent buffetings. In this way the loss of loved ones actually brings profit in its train, even though the passion may revolt against it ; and while the sedative may be bitter to the taste, yet it does in the end afford relief. It was such an idea as this the poet had in mind when he wrote :

In truth, though we have lost in thee our lord,
Our cave of refuge, and for thee
Have grieved and fretted long,
Yet hath our loss yielded this much reward :
We can outface calamity,
Though it be massive strong.

As for the man who prefers to follow the dictate of reason and to deny the call of passion, who has complete possession and control of himself, against grief he has one sure protection. The intelligent and perfect man never chooses to continue in a situation that is harmful to him, and therefore he is up betimes to reflect upon the cause of the grief whereby he has been visited. If it be a matter that can be repelled and put an end to, he substitutes for grieving a consideration of the means he may adopt to repel and put an end to that cause. If however it be a matter that cannot be treated after this fashion, he forthwith sets about diverting his mind from it and trying to forget it, striving to obliterate it from his thoughts and drive it out of his soul. This is because it is passion, not reason, that invites him to continue grieving in those circumstances ; for reason only urges one towards a course that yields profit sooner or later. But to grieve over what yields no return whatsoever, but only immediate loss, is bound, so far from proving profitable, to lead to yet further loss in the long run too. The intelligent and perfect man follows only the dictate of reason, and never continues in any state unless he feels free to do so for a definite reason and with a clear justification ; he will not follow or obey or go along with his passion when it would lead him in a contrary direction.

CHAPTER XIII

Of Greed

GREED and gluttony are among those evil dispositions that afterwards yield pain and mischief. For not only do they bring upon a man the contempt and vilification of his fellows ; they land him with indigestion into the bargain, and that leads on to all sorts of very serious ailments.

Greed is generated out of the force of the appetitive soul ; when this is reinforced and assisted by blindness of the rational soul—in other words lack of shame—it becomes apparent and revealed in addition. This too is a sort of following after passion ; it is brought on and stimulated by picturing the pleasure of tasting the food one is about to eat. I have been told of a greedy man who one day fell upon a variety of foods with extreme gluttony and greed ; when he was full and his sides were bursting, and he could not touch a single scrap more, he broke into tears. Questioned as to the reason for his weeping, he replied that it was because he was unable, as he averred, to eat any of the things before him. Again I remember I was eating once with a certain man in Baghdad, and a huge quantity of dates was put before us. I refrained from taking more than a moderate amount, but he persevered until he had very nearly finished the lot. When he was full and had given over eating, I noticed that he was goggling at the remainder as they were removed from the table ; and so I asked him whether his soul was satisfied and his appetite assuaged. He answered, " I only wish I could be in my former state again, and this plate be put before us right now!" I said to him, "If the pain and gnawing of desire have not left you even now, would it not be better to refrain before you are full, so as to relieve yourself at least of the heaviness and distention of being replete? The indigestion which you cannot be sure of not suffering is bound to bring upon you ailments that will be many, many times more painful for you than the pleasure you had in what you have taken." I saw that he understood my meaning, and that my words went home and did him good; and upon my life, such reasoning as this satisfies those who have not been trained in the discipline of philosophy, more than arguments based on philosophic principles.

This is because the man who believes that the appetitive soul is united with the rational soul only in order that it may supply this body, which serves the rational soul as an instrument and an implement, with sufficient to keep it alive for the period required by the rational soul to acquire knowledge of this world—such a man will always suppress the appetitive soul and prevent it from obtaining food above a modest adequacy. For he takes the view that the object and purpose of feeding in created beings is not enjoyment but survival, which cannot be secured without food. This is illustrated by the story of the philosopher who was eating with a youth wholly undisciplined. The latter expressed surprise at the small amount the philosopher was taking, saying among other things, "If my whack of food was only as much as yours, I would not care whether I was alive or not." The philosopher replied, "That is quite true, my son. I eat in order that I may live, whereas you only want to live in order that you may eat."

As for the man who sees no harm on religious or theoretical grounds in filling himself and taking as much food as possible, he should nevertheless be held back from doing so by the argument about balancing the pleasure so enjoyed against the consequent pain, as we have explained before. We would also add that since it is inevitable that the food which gives so much pleasure must be denied the eater in the end, it behoves the intelligent man to put forward the moment, before the situation arises where he cannot be sure of not being involved in evil consequences. For if he does not do this, he will lose and not gain at all, by exposing himself to pain and sickness : that is how he may lose, while his failure to gain is evidenced by the fact, that the mortification of being denied the pleasure of eating is in any case bound to overtake him some time. And if he departs from this rule or inclines in the opposite direction, let him be aware that he has dethroned his reason in favour of his passion.

Greed and gluttony are characterized besides by a great voracity and wolfishness ; if they are indulged and given their head, this element becomes extremely strong and it proves difficult to rid the soul of it, whereas if they are restrained and suppressed it grows weak and faint and feeble as time goes on, and finally disappears altogether. The poet says :

Know, that the use of hunger is a shield
And a protection, that doth riches yield ;
Whereas the habit of satiety
May stir a hunger fiercer yet in thee.

CHAPTER XIV

Of Drunkenness

CHRONIC and habitual drunkenness is one of the evil dispositions that bring those indulging it to ruin, calamity and all
kinds of sickness. This is because the excessive drinker is
imminently liable to apoplexy and asphyxia, that filling of
the inner heart which induces sudden death, rupture of the
arteries of the brain, and stumbling and falling into crevices
and wells ; not to mention various fevers, bloody clots and
bilious swellings in the intestines and principal parts, and
delirium tremens and palsy especially if there be a natural
weakness of the nerves. Besides all this, drunkenness leads
to loss of reason, immodesty, divulging of secrets, and a general
incapacity to grasp even the most important mundane and
spiritual matters ; so that a man will hardly hold on to any
cherished purpose or achieve any lasting happiness, but on
the contrary he will go on slipping and sliding downwards.
It was of such a situation that the poet wrote :

> When shall it be within thy power
> To grasp the good things God doth shower
> Though they be but a span from thee,
> If all thy nights in revelry
> Be passed, and in the morn thou rise
> With fumes of drinking in thine eyes
> And, heavy with its wind, ere noon
> Returnest to thy drunkard's boon ?

In short, drink is one of the most serious constituents of

passion, and one of the greatest disorders of the reason. That is because it strengthens the appetitive and choleric souls and sharpens their powers, so that they demand urgently and insistently that the drinker shall embark precipitately upon their favourite course. Drink also weakens the rational soul and stultifies its powers, so that it is scarcely able to undertake careful thought and deliberation but rushes headlong to a decision and liberates action before its energy is firmly established. Hence the rational soul is led on easily and smoothly by the appetitive soul, until it is scarcely able to resist it or deny it anything. This is the sign of a departure from rationality, and of enrolment in the order of beasts.

It therefore behoves the intelligent man to beware of drink, and to keep it in its proper place, namely that which is here indicated, fearing it as he would fear one who aims to rob him of his most prized and precious possessions. If he touches drink at all, he should do so only when anxiety and care oppress and overwhelm him. Moreover his purpose and intention should be not to seek pleasure for its own sake and to follow it wherever it may lead, but to reject superfluous pleasure and to indulge only so much as he is confident will not mischief him and upset his constitution. He should call to mind in this and similar situations our remarks on the suppression of passion, keeping before him a picture of these overall observations and general principles so that he may not need to remember them again and repeat them. In particular he should recall our statement that the constant and assiduous indulgence of pleasure diminishes our enjoyment thereof, reducing that to the position of something necessary for the maintenance of life.

This idea is almost more valid when applied to the pleasure of drunkenness than in the case of any other pleasure ; that is because the drunkard reaches a stage where he cannot conceive of living without drink, while sobriety is to him just like the state of a man beset by pressing cares. Moreover drunkenness is not less insatiable than greed ; indeed it is even very much more insatiable ; one must accordingly be equally swift to grapple with it and equally strenuous in reining and denying it.

Sometimes of course drink is a necessity, so as to dispel anxiety, and in other situations requiring excessive cheerfulness, courage, impetuosity and recklessness. Still it is proper to beware of it, and not to come near it at all in situations that need exceptional thought, a clear understanding and a steady resolve.

CHAPTER XV

Of Sexual Intercourse

THIS again is one of the evil dispositions stimulated and induced by passion and the preference for pleasure, involving the man indulging it in all kinds of calamities and evil disorders. It weakens the eyesight, undermines and wears out the body, brings on premature old age, senility and wasting, injures the brain and nerves, and reduces and weakens the strength ; quite apart from other ailments too numerous to mention. It is marked by an extreme voracity just like other pleasurable occupations—indeed it is more strongly and powerfully affected than the rest, because the soul remembers how excessively pleasurable it is compared with the others. In addition to this, frequent use of the sexual organ enlarges the testicles and attracts to them much blood, with the result that more and more sperm is generated in them ; so the lust and yearning to indulge augments and increases over and over again. Contrariwise, when one diminishes or refrains from intercourse, the body retains that original freshness which is the peculiar property of the substance of the members, with the result that the period of growth and development is extended and the processes of aging, drying up, emaciation and senility are retarded ; the testicles contract and cease to demand supplies ; the generation of sperm is diminished ; distention becomes slight ; the male organ recedes ; and the appetite falls away, so that its urge is no longer violent and its demands are no more pressing.

It therefore behoves the intelligent man to rein and restrain himself in this respect too, striving with his soul that it may not egg him on and excite him, lest it bring him to a state where it is difficult if not impossible to check and restrain it from indulgence. He should remember and keep in mind all that we have remarked on the reining and restraining of passion, especially our statement in the chapter on greed that the appetite rages and burns and incites and demands gratification even after it has attained and achieved the very limit of what it can possibly endure to enjoy. This is because this idea is even more valid and obvious when applied to the pleasure enjoyed in sexual intercourse than in the case of all other pleasures, because of the superiority it is pictured as having over the rest. For the soul—especially if it be neglected and left to its own devices, undisciplined, or what the philosophers call unrestrained—by no means finds its appetite diminished by the constant indulgence of the sexual urge, neither does frequent resort to concubines in any way lessen its desire and yearning for still others. And because this cannot be infinitely accomplished, such a man is inevitably burnt up by the flame and fire of thwarted enjoyment of the desired object; he suffers and endures the pain of deprivation, while the urge and incentive still rage within him; either for want of money and vigour, or through a natural and constitutional weakness and impotence. It is impossible in any case ever to attain as much gratification of the desired object as the lust demands and urges; as with the two men referred to in the chapter on greed.

This being so, the only right course lies in advancing the event which must in any case occur and be endured—namely the thwarting of enjoyment of the desired object while the incentive and urge still remain—before that enjoyment has been extensively and excessively indulged; in that way one can hope to be saved from its evil consequences, and avert its voracity and wolfishness and violent incitements and demands.

Besides all this, this particular pleasure is in any case the most proper and right of all pleasures to be cast away. This is because it is not necessary for the continuance of life, like eating and drinking, while there is no obvious and palpable pain in giving it up, like the pain of hunger and thirst ; whereas its excessive and immoderate indulgence destroys and demolishes the structure of the body. To obey its summons and to go along with it is a sure and certain sign that the passion has triumphed and obliterated the reason—and that is a state of affairs which the intelligent man ought certainly to disdain and rise superior to, not seeking to emulate stallion bucks and bulls and other beasts that are without deliberation and regard for the future.

Moreover the disapprobation evinced by the great majority of mankind for this business, their revulsion against it and the way they hide and conceal it when they do practise it, prove it to be a thing detested by the rational soul. For that general revulsion of men against this affair must be due either to a natural instinct or to education and training ; on either count, it is clear that it must be something revolting and evil in itself. That is because it is laid down in the laws of logic that opinions about whose soundness no doubt is to be entertained are those commonly held either by all or the majority or the wisest of mankind.

It is not incumbent upon us to persist in doing the thing that is revolting and hideous ; rather it is our duty to leave it alone altogether ; or, if we cannot avoid doing it, then we should do it as little as possible, and then with a due sense of shame and self-reproach. To act otherwise is to deny the reason and follow the inclinations of passion ; and anyone who so comports himself is reckoned by intelligent men to be baser than the animals, and more subservient to passion than even they, since he prefers to follow and obey the call of passion in spite of the fact that his reason informs and warns him of the disadvantages he will suffer in acting thus ; whereas the animal merely follows its natural instincts, having nothing to warn it, or inform it of the disadvantages resulting from its behaviour.

CHAPTER XVI

Of Excessive Fondness and Trifling, and Ritual

NOTHING further is required for the abandonment and giving up of these two—fondness and trifling [1]—than a sound resolve to do so, and a sense of shame and disdain for them ; reinforced by a habitual reminding of the soul to that effect on all occasions of trifling and inordinate fondness, until these two dispositions themselves act like the string tied about one's finger as a reminder. It is related of a certain king, a man of intelligence, that he was very fond and partial to trifling with some part of his body—I think it was his beard. This went on for a long time, despite the fact that he was constantly being told about it by a courtier ; it was as though some fit of absent-mindedness and forgetfulness always insisted that he should revert to the habit. Finally one of his ministers said to him one day, "Your Majesty, make a separate resolution to deal with this business, as sensible men do." The king blushed and became furiously angry, but he was never once observed to do that thing again. The man's rational soul had excited his choleric soul to pride and disdain, so that the resolve became sound and firm within his rational soul until it affected him powerfully and became a constant reminder to him, arousing him whenever he was heedless. And by my life, the only purpose for which the choleric soul was made is to assist the rational against the appetitive soul when the struggle is fierce, the attraction strong and the draw difficult to withstand.

[1] What we would call fidgeting and playing about with some part of oneself.

It behoves the intelligent man to be angry, and to be affected by disdain and pride, whenever he observes any appetite trying to dominate him and overcome his better judgment and his reason ; then he will humble and suppress it, obliging it perforce obsequiously to stand by the arbitrament of his reason. It would be strange, and indeed impossible, for a man who was able to rein his soul against following its lusts, despite their powerful urge and incitements, yet to find it difficult to prevent its giving in to fondness and trifling, which constitute no such great appetite and pleasure. Most of what is required to meet this situation is to be mindful and alert, for in most cases the trouble only occurs because of forgetfulness and absent-mindedness.

As for ritual,[1] this calls for merely a few words to demonstrate that it is an accident of the passion and not the intellect ; we shall therefore say something on this subject brief and to the point. Cleanliness and purity ought to be assessed only by the senses, not by analogy ; and matters therewith connected should be regulated according to the reach of the sensation, not of the imagination. If the senses fail to perceive any impurity in a thing, we call it pure ; if the senses fail to perceive any filth in a thing, we call it clean.

Now our object in desiring and intending these two conditions —purity and cleanliness—is either for the sake of religion or out of squeamishness ; and we are not injured in either of these respects by a little impurity or filth so trifling as to escape the senses. Thus, religion has sanctioned the performance of the ritual prayer while wearing a single garment that has been touched by the feet of flies which have fallen into blood and dung ; and purification by means of running water is recognized even though we may know that it has been staled, or by means

---

[1] Rhazes obviously here refers to such ritual practices as ablution.

of stagnant water in a large pool although we may know that it contains a drop of blood or wine. Nor does this injure us in regard to our sense of squeamishness, because obviously what escapes the senses cannot be perceived by us, and what we do not perceive, our spirits do not fear ; and what our spirits do not fear, there is no sense whatever in feeling squeamish about. Therefore we are not injured by impurity or filth so slight as to be swallowed up and not noticed ; it is not right that we should think about it, neither need its presence occur to our minds at all.

If however we go on looking for purity and cleanliness in full reality and exactitude, and treat the matter as touching our imagination and not our senses, we shall never find our way to anything that is pure and clean by this arbitrament. This is because we can never be sure regarding the water we use that it has not been filthied by human agency, or that the carcase of a reptile or wild or domestic animal or its dung or droppings has not fallen into it. If we pour and spray it over ourselves a great deal, we cannot be certain that the last rinse will not be the filthiest and impurest. Consequently God has not imposed the duty of self-purification upon His servants after this manner, for that would be something beyond our means and capability.

This it is that makes life intolerable to the man who has a squeamish fancy, because he cannot touch any food or approach anything and be quite sure that there is not some filth swallowed up there. If these matters are as we have described, the ritualist has no argument left to him ; and how deplorable it is for an intelligent man to make a stand over a point where he has no valid excuse or argument to support him ! That is the very abnegation of reason, and the pursuit of pure and unadulterated passion.

CHAPTER XVII

Of Earning, Acquiring and Expending

REASON, our especial gift whereby we have been preferred above the other irrational animals, has made it possible for us to enjoy a good life in mutual helpfulness. Rarely do we see beasts performing a like service for each other; and we observe that the agreeable circumstances of our life are due in the main to co-operation and mutual helpfulness. But for this, we should have no advantage in the way of a pleasant life over the brute beasts. For since the beasts have not perfected any system of co-operation and intellectual assistance such as that which organizes our life, the efforts of the many do not bring benefit to the individual with them, as we observe the case to be with man.

Each one of us eats, is clothed, has shelter, and is secure; yet the individual only prosecutes one of these businesses. If he is a husbandman, he cannot be a builder; if he is a builder, he cannot be a weaver; if he is a weaver, he cannot be a warrior. In short, if you could imagine a single man living alone in a waterless desert, perhaps you would not picture him as existing at all; and even were you to imagine him alive, you would scarcely picture his life as good and agreeable, such as that of one whose needs were all amply supplied and the requirements of his strivings adequately met; rather would you represent his life as wild, beastly and sordid. That is because he would lack that co-operation and mutual assistance which would confer on him a good and pleasant life and tranquillity.

When many men agree to co-operate and help each other, they parcel out the various sorts of profitable endeavour among themselves ; each labours upon a single business until he achieves its complete fulfilment, so that every man is simultaneously a servant and served, toiling for others and having others toiling for him. In this way all enjoy an agreeable life and all know the blessings of plenty ; even though there is a wide difference between them and an extensive variety of rank and accomplishment ; nevertheless there is not one who is not served and laboured for, or whose needs are not wholly sufficed.

Having prefixed what we thought good and necessary as a prelude to this chapter, we now return to our immediate object. Since human life can only be completely and effectively organized on the basis of co-operation and mutual help, it is the duty of every man to adhere to one or other of the means of providing this assistance, and to labour to the limits of his powers and abilities to that end, avoiding at the same time the two extremes of excess and deficiency. For one of these extremes—that is, deficiency—is vile baseness and mean worthlessness, since it brings a man down to the level of a pauper and a charge upon others ; while the other extreme involves labour without respite and slavery without term.

When a man desires his neighbour to give him something of his belongings without any exchange or compensation, he thereby debases himself and puts himself in the same position as one disabled by paralysis or accidental injury from earning his living. And when a man fixes no definite limit to his earning and is not prepared to restrict himself to such a limitation, the service he renders to his fellows is many times greater than their service to him, and he continues moreover in bondage and perpetual slavery ; for if he labours and toils all his life to earn more than he requires for his expenses and needs and to provide an adequate capital and reserve, he is really the loser in the long run, and is both deceived and enslaved without being aware of the fact. For men take wealth as a mark and a stamp whereby it is mutually recognized how much each deserves for his labour and the toil he performs that is profitable to all. Therefore when any one man is specially distinguished for amassing tokens by his toil and labour, and does not dispose of them in ways that will yield him repose, through the labour of his fellows to supply his needs, he is really the loser and has suffered himself to be deceived and enslaved; for he will have given away his own toil and effort without obtaining in compensation any adequate provision or repose. Such a man has not bartered toil against toil and service against service; the exchange he will have received is worthless and useless; his effort and toil and provision will have yielded profit to his fellows which they will have enjoyed, whereas their provision and toil on his account will have passed him by, and his enjoyment of their produce will be far less than the worth of his deserts seeing how he has provided and laboured for them. So he will have lost out and been deceived and enslaved, as we have stated. The true object in earning is therefore to gain as much as will balance the amount of one's expenditure, with something over to put away and keep in store against such emergencies and accidents as may prevent one from earning. The man who follows this rule in earning his living will have received in exchange toil for toil and service for service.

Now for a few words on the subject of acquisition. To acquire and store away is also one of the means necessary to the enjoyment of a good life, resting as it does upon a sound intellectual prognosis. The matter is too apparent and obvious to require an explanation ; even many animals that are not rational acquire and store away. It is more proper that such animals should have a superior mental imagination compared with those that are not acquisitive ; for the reason and motive for such acquisition is the picturing of a situation in which the object acquired may be lost while the need for it still remains. All the same it may be necessary to observe moderation in this, according to what we have stated in our discussion on the quantity of earning : deficiency may lead to its complete non-existence while the need still exists, as for instance with a man whose provisions are exhausted while he is in a waterless desert, while excess may have the same result as incessant toil and exhaustion, after the fashion we have described. The just medium in regard to acquisition is for a man to be able to have recourse to what he has acquired, sufficient to support him in his continuing circumstances at a time when an accident may occur preventing him from earning.

As for the man whose purpose in acquiring is to move himself out of the circumstances in which he finds himself, into a higher and grander state, and who never sets any limit on this to which he will strictly confine himself : such a man continues in perpetual toil and bondage, and lacks withal—whatever be his original state—any enjoyment or happiness in the state to which he moves, since he still goes on toiling and is never satisfied. He is always working to shift himself into another, higher state, yearning and hankering after attaching himself to yet grander circumstances. This we have stated in the chapter on envy, and we shall give a clearer and fuller explanation and account of the matter in the section following this.

The best possible acquisition, at once the most lasting, the most respectable and the securest, is a profession, especially if it be a natural and necessary one which is always and constantly in demand in every country and among all nations. Properties, precious things, treasures are not secure against the accidents of time, and therefore the philosophers have reckoned no man rich in respect of his properties, but only in regard to his profession. It is told how a certain philosopher was shipwrecked at sea, and lost all his belongings, but when he came to shore he saw on the ground the drawing of a geometrical design; and he rejoiced because he knew that he had fallen upon an island where there were learned people. He obtained wealth and a position of leadership amongst them, and remained there. Ships afterwards passed by, making for his native land, and they asked him whether there was any message they could carry for him to his people. He replied, " When you come to them, say to them, Acquire and store away that which cannot be sunk."

As for the quantity of expenditure : we have mentioned before that the amount of earning must be equivalent to the amount of spending, with a little bit over acquired and stored away for accidents and emergencies. The amount of expenditure must therefore obviously be less than the amount of earning. All the same, a man ought not to be so moved by the inclination to acquire that he is parsimonious and cheeseparing, or so carried away by the love and pursuit of his appetites that he gives up acquiring altogether. Every man should observe moderation in this matter, according to the amount he earns, his habits of expenditure, the manner of life he has been brought up to, his actual circumstances, his position in society, and what it behoves a man like himself to acquire and store away.

CHAPTER XVIII

Of the Quest for Worldly Rank and Station

WE have already put out earlier in various chapters of this book some general statements of what is required in the present chapter ; however, in view of the lofty purpose aimed at in this chapter and its very great usefulness, we propose to devote a separate discussion to this particular subject, gathering together the different points and ideas that have gone before, and adding to these some further observations which we think will help to achieve and complete our object.

If any man desires to ornament and ennoble his soul with this virtue, and to release and relieve it from imprisonment and bondage, and the manifold cares and sorrows that visit him and deliver him over to passion—that passion which urges him to pursue an object diametrically opposed to the purpose intended in this chapter—if this be his desire, it behoves him in the first place to remember and keep in mind what we have already remarked on the superiority of reason and rational action ; and then our statement on the reining and suppressing of desire, and its subtle deceits and traps. He should also recall our description and definition of pleasure ; after which he should diligently deliberate and meditate and unremittingly study what we have written in the chapter on envy, where we said that the intelligent man ought to consider the various circumstances of his fellows. He ought further to study what we have stated at the beginning of the chapter on the repelling of grief. When he thoroughly knows and understands all

G*

these things, and they are firmly fixed and established in his soul, let him finally proceed to comprehend what we are about to remark in this place.

Because of the faculty we possess of dramatization and intellectual analogy, it often happens that we picture to ourselves the consequences and issues of various affairs, so that we sense and perceive them as though they had actually happened. Then if these are hurtful we turn away from them, whereas if they are profitable we make haste to realize them. Upon this fact depends in the main the good life we enjoy, as well as our immunity from those things that are harmful, evil and destructive. It therefore behoves us to respect and reverence this virtue, making use of it and summoning it to our aid ; we ought to conduct our affairs according to its guidance. For it is a way to salvation and safety, and distinguishes us above the beasts that pursue impetuously paths whose end and issue they cannot visualize.

Let us therefore consider, with the eye of reason unclouded by passion, the question of removing from one set of circumstances to another and from a lower rank to a higher, in order that we may ascertain which is the better and more restful and reasonable state to seek and cleave to. We will make this our point of departure in the present investigation.

These so-called states may be enumerated as three—our present continuing state in which we have grown up and been nurtured, that which is grander and higher, and that which is lower and meaner. That the soul, at first blush and without reflection or consideration, prefers and loves and clings to the state that is grander and higher, this much we can discover from examining ourselves ; yet we cannot be sure that we are not being motivated by the inclination and impetuosity of desire rather than the arbitrament of reason. Let us accordingly marshal our arguments and proofs, and then pass our verdict as they require.

To remove out of the state to which we have always been used and accustomed into grander circumstances can only be the result—if we except rare and wonderful accidents—of driving oneself, and the most strenuous endeavour. Let us therefore consider also whether it is really right for us to press and exhaust ourselves, in order to rise to a grander state than what we have been accustomed to or what our bodies have been familiar with. On this point we would observe that if a man's body has grown and reached maturity, while he has never been accustomed to be treated as a person of authority, with retinues going before and after him, and if he then strains and strives to achieve that state, he stands convicted of having turned away from reason to follow passion. For he can never attain such a rank, except by toil and violent effort and by driving himself to face dangers and take risks and put himself in jeopardy, in short to do those things which in the majority of cases lead to ruin ; neither will he succeed in his ambition, without bringing upon himself suffering many times greater than the pleasure he will stand to enjoy after achieving his goal. In that case he is merely deceived and deluded by the picture he has drawn of reaching his object, without forming any image of the road whereby alone he can come to it ; so we have explained in our discussion of pleasure. And when he has at last attained and achieved his cherished desire, it is not long before he loses all happiness and enjoyment of it ; for his new circumstances become like all other customary and usual conditions. Consequently the pleasure he feels in his new life rapidly diminishes, while he finds himself loaded with increasingly heavy burdens in the effort to maintain and preserve his advance. Passion will not in any case allow him to abandon or give up his achievements—so we showed when we were speaking of the reining of passion—so that in fact he has gained nothing and lost many things. He has gained nothing, because once he is used and habituated to those new circumstances they become exactly the same to him as his original position, so that he ceases to feel any joy and happiness in them. He has lost many things, on account of the weariness in the first place, and the danger and hazard he runs in struggling to the new state, and in the second place because of the effort to keep it, the fear of losing it, the grief if it should be gone, and the stress of habituating himself to living and wanting to live in such circumstances.

We would make the same comment on every set of circumstances beyond a modest sufficiency. For if the body is accustomed to a rough diet and commonplace clothes, and if one then struggles to change these for delicate food and fine raiment, the extreme pleasure a man feels in achieving these falls away once he is used to them, so that in the end they become exactly the same to him as what he had originally; while all that he has gained is the extra toil and effort to attain and preserve these amenities, the fear of being deprived of them, and the labour of getting used to them—from all of which disadvantages he was previously exempt.

We have the same remarks to offer on power, position, renown, and all other worldly ambitions. There is no rank whatever that one can reach or achieve, but that the happiness and enjoyment of its attaining every day grows less and diminishes until it finally vanishes altogether. So any rank whatsoever comes in the end to mean no more to him who attains it than the station he left to mount up to it, and all he gains for the sake of his ambition is extra trouble, worry, care and grief such as he never knew in the past. For he still continues to think little of the position he is actually occupying, and to struggle to mount up yet higher, while he never reaches a station completely satisfying to his soul once he has won through and become established there. It may be indeed that before he arrives, his passion represents him as satisfied and content with the conditions at which he is aiming ; but that is one of passion's greatest deceits and weapons and traps, to spur him on and draw him forward to the cherished goal ; once he has arrived at his destination, he at once gazes up at a still loftier reach. That is the condition he finds himself in, so long as he associates with and is obedient to his passion. We have made statements to this effect elsewhere in this book, representing this to be one of passion's greatest snares and delusions. For in such circumstances passion appears to a man in the semblance of reason, camouflaging itself and making him imagine that its appeal is that of the reason and not of the passion at all ; it represents to him that the vision it is granting him is of virtue, not lust, so that it makes some show of intellectual argument and satisfaction. But the satisfaction and argument do not prevail long ; when they are collated with straightforward reasoning, they are soon confounded and disproved.

The discourse on the difference between reasoned and passionate representation is an important topic of the art of logical demonstration, which however it is not necessary to introduce in this context ; we have already adumbrated it in more than one place in our present book, quite sufficiently for our purpose. Moreover we propose to set out a few of its headings in enough detail to enable us to attain our actual object in this book.

Reason represents, chooses and desires always that course which is preferable, nobler and more salutary in the issue, even though it may to begin with impose upon the soul trouble, hardship and difficulty. Passion is exactly the opposite of this, in that it always chooses and prefers the immediate, contiguous and adherent impulse of the moment, even though its consequences may be harmful, without any consideration or reflection of what comes after. An instance of this is the case we mentioned when we were discussing the reining of the passion, that of the boy with ophthalmia who preferred to eat dates and play in the sun rather than take myrobalan [1] and submit to cupping and the usual treatment for eye-disease. Reason represents what is to one's advantage as well as what is hurtful to one, whereas passion always shows one what is advantageous and blinds one to the rest. For example, a man will be blind to his own faults, while seeing his few virtues as greater than they really are. It therefore behoves the intelligent man always to suspect his judgment in matters that seem to his advantage and not to his detriment, and to suppose that his opinion is influenced by passion not reason ; he should investigate such matters very thoroughly before he acts.

Reason supports its representations with argument and clear justification, while passion satisfies and represents merely on the basis of inclination and congeniality, not with argument that can be logically stated and expressed. Sometimes passion fastens on to a certain show of logic, as when it sets out to assume the semblance of reason ; but its argument is hesitant and interrupted, and its justification is neither obvious nor clear. Examples of this are available in the cases of the lovers, those seduced by intoxication or bad and hurtful food, ritualists, men who habitually pluck out their beards, and those who trifle or are inordinately fond of some part of their bodies. Ask some of these to justify their conduct, and they will not

[1] " The astringent fruit of certain Indian mountain species of *Terminalia* " (Chambers).

have a word to say ; the only argument they will be able to muster will amount to no more than that such is their inclination, that they find it congenial, or that they like doing it—an instinctive, not a logical liking, mark you. Some of them indeed begin to argue and say something, but as soon as they are refuted they relapse into repetition and meaningless drivel ; presently things get too much for them and they become furious ; under pressure they are unable to speak ; finally, having been silenced, they are cured.

These few headings are sufficient in this context, to prove the necessity of being on one's guard against passion and ignorantly going along with it.

We have shown how advancement to high rank involves effort and danger, and means casting oneself into circumstances that yield only a little happiness and joy, while experiencing such troubles and hardships as one was wholly exempt from in one's original state—evils that cannot be extricated and withdrawn from. It has been made clear that the most salutary state is that of a modest adequacy, and to reach after that in the easiest possible way, the manner most secure as to its sequel. We must prefer this state, and continue in it, if we wish to be people who are intellectually happy, and to avoid the troubles that lurk and lie in wait for those who pursue and prefer passion ; and if we desire to profit to the full of our human advantage— the gift of reason, by which alone we are distinguished above the beasts. If however we are unable to control passion so completely as to cast away from us all that is superfluous to that modest competence, at least those of us who possess such superfluity should limit themselves to their usual and accustomed state, and not exert and drive themselves and risk their lives to move upwards. Even if it should be within our power to attain a grand position without any labour or hazard, yet it is better and more salutary not to suffer ourselves to remove into it ; for we should not be free of those troubles which we have enumerated as consequentially befalling us after reaching and attaining the desired rank. If we did in fact move into those new circumstances, it must be on condition that we do not change any of our former habits and customs in eating, drinking, clothing ourselves, and all the other bodily requisites. Unless we do this, we shall find ourselves presently accustomed to superfluous extravagance, and in a state that makes demands upon us to live up to our new situation even should we lose it. Unless we do this, we shall experience extreme sorrow in the loss of these advantages when such loss comes upon us. Finally, we shall have deserted reason to join the ranks of passion, and therefore we shall fall into those very calamities which we have described.

CHAPTER XIX

Of the Virtuous Life

THE life which has been followed by all the great philosophers of the past may be described in a few words : it consists in treating all men justly. Thereafter it means acting nobly towards them, with a proper continence, compassion, universal benevolence, and an endeavour to secure the advantage of all men ; save only those who have embarked upon a career of injustice and oppression, or who labour to overthrow the constitution, practising those things which good government prohibits—disorder, mischief and corruption.

Now many men are constrained by their evil laws and systems to live a life of wrongdoing ; such are the followers of Daisan,[1] the Red Khurramis,[2] and others who hold it lawful to act deceitfully and treacherously towards their opponents ; or the Manicheans with their refusal to give water or food to those who do not share their opinions or to treat them medically when they are ill, who abstain from killing snakes, scorpions and suchlike noisome creatures which cannot possibly be expected to be of use or to be turned to any profitable purpose whatsoever, and who decline to purify themselves with water. Many men, I say, are of this persuasion and do various things, some of which result in mischief to the community as a whole, while some are hurtful to the practitioner himself. Such men cannot be won from their evil manner of life, except by serious

[1] An early heresiarch.
[2] A branch of the Khurrami sect, heretics of the ninth century.

discourse on opinions and doctrines ; and that discussion far transcends the scope and purpose of this book.

There is nothing left for us to say on this subject, therefore, further than to recall the kind of life which, when strictly followed, will secure a man from the hurt of his fellows, and will earn him their love.   So we assert that if a man cleaves to justice and continence, and allows himself but rarely to quarrel and contend with his fellows, he will in the main be safe from them.   If to this he adds goodness and benevolence and mercy in his dealings with others, he will win their love.   These two attributes are the reward of the virtuous life ; and what we have said is sufficient for our purpose in this book.

CHAPTER XX

Of the Fear of Death

THIS disposition cannot be expelled from the soul entirely, except it be satisfied that it will pass after death into a state more salutary to it than its present. Now this is a topic which calls for an extremely long discussion, if it be sought by way of logical demonstration and not mere report; and there is no possibility of such a discussion, especially in this book, because as we have said before its content exceeds the content of this alike in loftiness, breadth and length. For it would need a consideration of all the religions and sects which believe and require that man will have a certain estate after death, and passing verdict thereafter in favour of those which are true and against those which are false. It is no secret that the purport of this matter is very difficult, and needs and must have a long discussion. We shall therefore put this aside, and turn our attention to satisfying those who hold and believe that the soul perishes with the corruption of the body; for as long as a man continues to fear death he will turn away from reason to follow after passion.

Man, according to these, will after death be affected by no pain whatsoever; for pain is a sensation, and sensation is a property only of the living being, who during the state of his life is plunged and saturated in pain. Now the state in which there is no pain is obviously more salutary than the state in which pain exists; death is therefore more salutary to man than life.

If it be objected that man, even though he be afflicted during his lifetime by pain, nevertheless also experiences pleasures which will not fall to him after death, the reply to this is a question : will he feel pain, or will he care or be troubled in any way whatever when he is in that state, merely because he cannot enjoy any pleasure ? If the answer to this be no—and so it is bound to be, because if this response is not given the implication will be that a man is alive even when he is dead— then it may be observed again that pain affects only the living and not the dead ; and so the objection is met by the remark that man will not be troubled by the fact that he cannot enjoy any pleasure. This being so, the argument returns to the point where it started, namely that the state of death is the more salutary.

For the factor which you supposed proved the advantage of the living over the dead is pleasure, and the dead have no need or yearning for pleasure, neither are the dead pained at not attaining it as are the living. Hence the living have no advantage over the dead ; for advantage can only be spoken of in the case of two parties being in need of a certain thing, when one of the parties possesses the advantage while the need still exists ; but when the thing needed is a matter of indifference, the advantage disappears. This being so, we return once more to the proposition that the state of death is the more salutary.

If it now be objected that these ideas cannot be applied to the dead, because they do not exist so far as the dead are concerned, we reply that we did not say that these ideas existed for them ; on the contrary, we merely posited them as imaginary and fictitious, to have a standard of analogy and comparison. When this line is denied to you, you are finished according to the laws of logic : this is a well-known variety

of termination which is called by logicians "applying the
closure", because the opponent closes the discourse and runs
away from it, not attempting to carry it on any further for
fear of having the verdict go against him. Even if he has
resort to repetition and saying the same things all over again,
the ultimate result is the same.

Know, that the verdict of reason that the state of death is
more salutary than the state of life depends upon the belief a
man has in the soul ; it may nevertheless happen that he will
continue to follow his passion in this matter. For the difference
between passionate and rational opinion is that the former is
chosen and preferred and clung to not on account of any
obvious proof or clear justification, but out of a sort of inclination towards that opinion, a sense of congeniality and affection
for it in the soul ; whereas the latter is chosen on obvious
proof and clear justification, even though the soul may revolt
against it and turn away from it.

Again, what is this so much desired and coveted pleasure ?
Is it anything else in reality than repose from that which causes
pain, as we have already demonstrated ? If this be so, only
the ignorant man will picture it as something to be sought
after and desired ; for he who enjoys repose from pain is
indifferent to that repose which, when it follows pain, is called
pleasure.

Furthermore if it be true, as we have proved before, that it
is superfluous to grieve over what must inevitably come to
pass, and if death be a thing that must inevitably happen, to
grieve over the fear of it is superfluous, whereas to divert
one's thoughts from it and to forget it is a manifest gain. It
is on this account that we have always admired the beasts in
this respect, because they possess by nature this kind of attitude
to perfection, whereas we cannot hope to achieve it save by

contriving to get rid of intellectual thought and imagination. And it would seem that that is the most profitable course to follow in this context ; for speculation on death brings upon us many times greater pain than that which is to be expected. The man who imagines death, and is afraid of it, dies a separate death at every image he calls up, so that his imagination over a long period concentrates upon him many deaths. Therefore the best and most advantageous course, for the peace of our souls, is gently but firmly to contrive to expel this grief from us. This agrees with what we have said before, that the intelligent man never grieves ; for if there be any cause for his grief that can be averted, instead of grieving he thinks about how to avert the cause of his grief, whereas if it be something that cannot be averted, he forthwith sets about diverting his thoughts and consoling himself, and strives to obliterate it and drive it out of his soul.

Again I repeat that I have demonstrated that there is no ground for fearing death, if a man holds that there is no future state after death. And now I say that in accordance with the other view—the view that makes out a future state attendant upon death—there is also no need for a man to fear death, if he be righteous and virtuous, and carries out all the duties imposed upon him by the religious law which is true ; for this law promises him victory and repose and the attainment of everlasting bliss. And if any man should doubt the truth of that law, or is ignorant of it, or is not certain that it is real, it only behoves him to search and consider to the limit of his strength and power ; for if he applies all his capacity and strength, without failing or flagging, he can scarcely fail to arrive at the right goal. And if he should fail—which is scarcely likely to happen—yet Almighty God is more apt to forgive and pardon him, seeing that He requires of no man what lies not within his capacity ; rather does He charge and impose upon His servants far, far less than that.

Since we have now achieved the purpose of our present book, and reached the end of our intention, we will end our discourse by giving thanks to our Lord. Infinite praise be unto God, the Giver of every blessing and Reliever of every perplexity, in accordance with His eternal worth and merit.

INDEX